Do We *Have* to Know This for the Exam?

By the same author

Coping in Medical School
Coping With Your Doctor

Do We *Have* to Know This for the Exam?

A Guide to Coping in College

BERNARD VIRSHUP, M.D.

ILLUSTRATIONS BY RICHARD LOUDERBACK

W · W · NORTON & COMPANY
New York   London

The text of this book is composed in Trump, with display type set in
Trump Gravure. Composition and manufacturing by the Haddon Craftsmen,
Inc.
Book design by Jacques Chazaud.

First Edition

ISBN 0-393-02408-3

ISBN 0-393-30391-8 PPK

W. W. Norton & Company, Inc. 500 Fifth Avenue, New York, N. Y. 10110
W. W. Norton & Company Ltd., 37 Great Russell Street, London WC1B
3NU

1 2 3 4 5 6 7 8 9 0

Contents

Appreciation   9
Introduction   13

1 Caring Relationships   21
2 Let's Talk about Sex
      (by Jacqueline Kansky)   38
3 Listening   50
4 Self-Awareness   62

  5 Self-Esteem   79
  6 Criticism   102
  7 Confidence   118
  8 Motivation   132
  9 Coping with Bad Feelings   155
 10 Anxiety   173
 11 Anger   191
 12 Depression   215
 13 Creative Coping   226
 14 Pathways   254

     APPENDIX A   Keeping a Journal   259
     APPENDIX B   Jungian Types   265
     INDEX   271
     YOUR PERSONAL JOURNAL   281

Do We *Have* to Know This for the Exam?

Appreciation

Some of us were sitting around a table after dinner, and the conversation turned to what we had learned in college outside the classroom. As we traded experiences, someone said, "Wouldn't it have been great if we could have known then what we know now?"

There was a chorus of agreement. "If I'd only known..."; "I made so many mistakes . . ."; "I could have . . ."

But one person disagreed. "It's easy to look back and

think, 'If only, 'If only,' but could you really have learned from others?''

I thought about that. "I don't know. I can remember a lot of times when someone's help could have saved me a lot of grief."

"Perhaps, if you would have listened, but would you have listened? Can one person learn this sort of thing from another? Maybe we have to learn from our own bad experiences."

"Well yes, I agree we learn from our own experiences. But couldn't we have been helped? Couldn't it have been less painful? We might even have come out of it better people."

"You might be right," she said. "Why don't you write a book and see if they'll listen?"

So I did.

Much of this book evolved through many such discussions, especially with my students at the University of Southern California Medical School and, more recently, the Art Center College of Design, as we listened, shared, suggested, disagreed, rethought, argued, explained, and clarified. Especially helpful were Dwaine Lawrence and Julie Nyquist, faculty at USC, friends who made me feel they were truly interested as we endlessly explored ideas. Then there was Hanna Weg in her junior year at Yale who painstakingly scrutinized an early version, made excellent suggestions, and saved me from embarrassingly out-of-date expressions. Mary Cunnane, "my" editor, conceived of the project, and spent a great deal of time helping me rethink, rewrite, and reorganize. John Ware was warmly supportive and more friend than agent. I learned a great deal from my sons, Steven, Gary and David, who were patiently tolerant as my ideas changed and evolved ("But last month you said . . .'') It seems to have worked out O.K.; they all enjoyed college, and are launched into interesting, challenging, and rewarding careers. Finally, I want to thank my wife and best friend Evelyn, who proofed innumerable enthusiastic revisions, insisted on clear language and illustrations, and generally supported, encouraged, and approved.

Thank you all.

Bernard Virshup
March 29, 1987

Introduction

When you first went off to college, you undoubtedly were happy with anticipation, excited about leaving the restrictions of home, and still somewhat apprehensive of the unknown. You might have seen *Revenge of the Nerds* and *Animal House*, but of course you knew college isn't like that. What you did know about college probably wasn't much help. Problems arose that you couldn't possibly have anticipated.

Most problems you can handle by yourself without too much difficulty, but occasionally one may arise which you'd like to talk over with someone sympathetic and knowledgeable. Perhaps, even though you will work most things out by yourself, I might be able to help somewhat by showing you some coping skills you can use when things get tough.

You may have noticed that some people handle stressful situations more effectively and with less anxiety or strain than others. Good copers have good coping skills, good ways of solving difficult problems. Not that there are *right* or *wrong* coping skills, there are just different coping skills, some of which will work better for you at times than others. If you know about them, you can use what is best for you. Most people aren't familiar with too many different ways of dealing with problems. A hammer is a very good tool to learn to use well; it will crack nuts, and open packages from home, and you can even part your hair with it, but no matter how skillful you are, it is not the best tool for every occasion.

Good coping is a *process,* a *way* of meeting situations that will lead to lasting satisfaction and enjoyment. Coping is a process by which you make one decision rather than another; a process by which you choose one pathway in life rather than another. Coping does not mean getting through the moment, muddling through, or getting by. It also does not mean getting the best grades in the school, or being voted Most Valuable Player, although that might be the result. Coping does not even mean just making the right decision; that can happen by chance. Coping means learning *how* to make the decisions that will be right for you in the long run.

What is that process? How can you tell which path is better? How do you know which decision is more likely to lead to success? Your life may depend on the decisions and pathways you are taking now. In this book we will look at some of the problems you, as a college student, are likely to encounter that may be difficult for you or cause you pain, and we will talk about various ways of coping with them. That doesn't mean I will give you the answers. In the first place, I don't have answers. In fact, I don't believe there are such things as "answers" to problems, and I don't believe much in books or people who do give answers to problems. I don't think there are right ways to do things, or that someone else can tell you what is right for you.

What I can do is to give you some additional information and ideas, and perhaps suggest ways of looking at your problems that you might not have thought of before. That doesn't mean that these ways will be best for you, only that they may give you additional options.

An important part of college is learning how to find your own way. You must decide for yourself if the information in books applies to you, and if so, how best to use it. After you have thought about it for a while, you may see your way more clearly. And it will be *your* way.

When you first go to college, you are changing many things in your life. You are leaving the caring discipline of your parents, and taking charge of your own life. You might not have agreed with all the rules of your parents, and opinions about how you should live, but you knew what they were. Now, you are on your own, and responsible for your own decisions. It is not so easy being your own boss. You may miss them more than you thought you would, their love, their rules, their voices . . . you may become homesick.

And you will have left behind many friends, with whom you used to share your thoughts and feelings. Making new friends can be easy sometimes. More often it is hard, especially if you suffer from shyness, and for awhile you may feel very lonely.

You will have decisions to make about sex. Our society sends a lot of mixed messages that can be confusing and hard to sort out. How do you safely find out what you like, what you don't like, what makes you feel joyous or guilty? Will you like yourself later? How can you be emotionally comfortable, assess consequences, plan healthy sex, take responsibility back from others, become a separate, unique, sexual being?

You may fall in love. That can be a wonderful experience. It can also be gut-wrenching. And if it ends badly, it can be suicidally depressing.

It is natural to want to "look good." Since we all want approval and respect, we tend to fashion an image that we think others will like. But will you lose the real you? Who is the "real you?" What does that mean? Is there such a person? How do you find out? We will talk about some exercises that will help you develop a heightened awareness of who you are and your own uniqueness and worth. If you wish you may even delve into your own unconscious and explore a little. The result will sometimes please you and sometimes upset you, but it will almost always surprise you, and may even help you find your way.

There are many ways in college to feel good or bad

about yourself. There are many ways you can decide whether or not you are a good and worthwhile person. You may believe you are only as good as your latest grade. Then that you must spend your life studying harder and doing better, and generally proving yourself through your performance. You may develop "performance anxiety," freeze in tests, fail to measure up to your own standards, and generally feel inadequate. Or your self-esteem may depend on what other people say about you, or whether they like you, so that you may constantly try to please everyone (and so please no one).

Without high self-esteem it is hard to be assertive and to speak up for yourself. People who are nonassertive don't get what they need because they have too much trouble asking for what they want. If you act like a rug, talk like a rug, and look like a rug, people will almost certainly walk on you. Waiting for others to take care of you when you don't say what you want for yourself is almost certain to leave you not taken care of. And that makes it very hard to feel good about yourself.

When you are not feeling good about yourself, it is especially hard to accept criticism. Of course, no one likes to be criticized, but most teaching is by feedback; your teacher asks something, and you answer, and the teacher comments and corrects. If you are defensive you can't use criticism; it is too unsettling. If you interpret it to mean that you are stupid, inadequate, and hopeless; that you should get things right the first time and never make mistakes; and that everyone is laughing at you—well, that makes it hard to stay interested in your work and keep your self-esteem.

And other students will also be ready to give you advice. After all, you will all want to help each other, and when students see you doing things that they think may get you into trouble, they will often point it out. How are you to deal with that? Besides, not all criticism is constructive; sometimes you will run into people, even teachers, who consciously or unconsciously take pleasure in putting you down. Not everyone at college is your friend, and it pays to be able to take care of yourself.

Sometimes, no matter how competent you are, things will go wrong. People you like won't like you; the ball will slip out of your fingers; assignments won't make sense; and you will find your confidence slipping. Sooner or later, it happens to everyone. There will be black hours when you experience the agony of self-doubt. You may come to the conclusion that you are incompetent, inadequate, and worthless; that you don't have the "right stuff."

And there will be times when, sitting at your desk with books piled up on either side and hours of studying ahead, you find that your mind keeps wandering, so that you look at the same page for fifteen minutes without knowing what you've been reading. The subject matter is dry and tasteless, and you wonder what you are doing in college. Your motivation is gone; you're not able to make yourself do what you should. You're burning out.

Throughout college you will have many feelings. Some of your feelings will be wonderful and joyous. That's great. But many of your feelings won't be so great. Loneliness, embarrassment, low self-esteem, self-doubt and self-blame, anxiety, anger, depression: these, and many other painful feelings will sometimes engulf you. All students, all people, experience them. You may think you are the only one feeling that way, and so add embarrassment, shame, or guilt to an already heavy load. Think again and look around you. *Everyone* has such feelings. They may not show them openly, but they have them just the same.

What are you to do when you have such feelings? Do you blame yourself? Think there is something wrong with you? Tell yourself to "snap out of it?" You can also deny, suppress, repress, displace, and otherwise avoid these feelings. Don't tell anyone, laugh a lot, pretend you feel fine. You can relieve them for a few hours with alcohol, drugs, food, overwork, and antisocial behaviors.

There is a message we hear that if we are not happy, there is something wrong with us, and we have available a wide range of medications and drugs to take so that we don't have to feel unhappy: uppers, downers, tranquilizers, sedatives, alcohol, mood-alterers, mind-benders, psychedelics, narcotics—all to make us "feel better."

And when they stop working, what then? Suicide? It crosses many people's minds. Many act on it. A lot of young people have. It certainly works. Nothing hurts after that. But I know there are better, less permanent ways of dealing with painful feelings. The very worst circumstances and frustrations can even result in a stronger personality, if you learn to deal with them well.

Who Helps You Cope With Stress?

To help you deal with these problems, most schools have counseling centers, staffed by experienced and reliable professionals. It is a resource available to you, and can be enormously rewarding. But it is up to you to get yourself there. Of course, you will handle most of your problems yourself, but there are concerned, experienced professionals who want to help. If you are not happy and want someone to talk to, they are available for you. Use them. There are no rewards for keeping a stiff upper lip and enduring in silence.

Learning how to cope well with these problems will lead to a successful, enjoyable college career. After all, these could be the happiest years of your life. If something is wrong, don't wait until next year. The life you save may be your own.

1 Caring Relationships

There was a very special "Peanuts" cartoon several years ago in which Charlie Brown's little sister asked him, "What is it like to be grown-up?" He answered, "Do you remember when you fell asleep in the car coming home, and Daddy carried you upstairs, and Mommy undressed you and put you to bed? Well, when you're grown-up, that never happens anymore." And they both looked sadly into the future.

College is certainly an exciting experience. It is also challenging. You are assuming responsibility for yourself, and taking charge of your own life. But exciting as it may be, it is also stressful. There will be pressures on you that will sometimes bend you out of shape. But of course, these pressures are important for growth; they help you develop psychological muscle. You will end up a stronger person.

The very first stress you will encounter will be that of leaving your family and friends behind. At first, the separation may hurt them more than you. Watching you eagerly go into your new life, they may turn their heads to hide their tears. At first, you will have so much to do, you will be too busy to think about them. But after the first few days, you will start missing them. In fact, this feeling of missing them may become very strong. As you experience loneliness, confusion, and anxiety, you may develop an overwhelming desire to go home. You may think there is something wrong with you.

There isn't anything wrong with you. You have become "homesick." It is perfectly natural for this to happen, when you are separated from your previous support system. Separation anxiety and depression are common and normal. It is not a weakness. We are all social beings who have learned to depend on the support of others for our emotional well-being. Especially when you are stressed, hurt, or lonely, the need for nurturing can become very strong. When that support is removed, we can have not only heartache, but headaches, stomachaches, and colds. Homesickness is an important cause of visits to the school doctor.

If this happens to you, there are at least three things you can do.

1. Call home. Don't be afraid to let your parents know how unhappy you are. They have been through this too. They will understand and not think the worse of you. Call your old friends. If some people you know came to the same college, go visit them. You might schedule an emergency trip home, or perhaps your parents or friends could come to visit you. Write a lot of letters, and exchange photographs. Put their pictures up on the wall. Stay in touch with your past as much as possible.

2. Acknowledge your feelings. That is, don't pretend to yourself that you don't have these feelings; don't shove them so far down that they are out of sight. Reassure yourself that this has nothing to do with your worth as a person; you're still O.K. And don't let these feelings get in the way of getting on with life. In spite of these feelings, do what has to be done. Take care of yourself; eat; keep yourself neat and well-dressed; go to classes and do your homework. This can be an important learning experience, that you can have painful feelings and still be O.K., still function.

3. Most important, get on with the business of making new relationships. There is life after separation. Life will never stop being a series of separations and growth, so this is an important lesson to learn.

If, in spite of everything, you get so homesick that you become depressed, call your counseling center. We'll talk more about depression later, but don't wait to get help; call now.

Loneliness

Eventually the feeling of homesickness will pass, and you will begin to establish new friends, new caring relationships. Some people seem to need a lot of friends; others need just one or two good friends with whom they can share their deepest thoughts and feelings. Whichever style fits you better is right for you. But everyone needs friends to help cope with life. Otherwise, college can be very lonely.

At a time of your life when relationships are especially important to you, the lack of a relationship, or the breaking up of one, can feel like a first order catastrophe. Having left home and the close friendships you had there, your new relationships are important. Since few relationships are calm and stable, loneliness afflicts all college students at one time or another, and indeed, people of all ages.

People have a wide range of feelings about loneliness. Some feel lonely in a roomful of people, and others never feel lonely, even when they are alone. The feeling has to do with what you need from people, and what your expectations are. Being alone is not the same thing as being lonely. People are all around you. The problem is making "people-connections" that fill your needs, and make you feel good.

Making New Networks

A network of friends can be quite difficult to achieve in college. A caring network that will fit *your* needs won't always happen just by chance. You may have to *make* it happen. How can you do this?

Let us talk briefly about opportunities. You must start by making yourself available to others. You start just by smiling and saying "Hello." There are people you will meet just by being in the same room with them, where you live, where you eat, where you go to class. You will pass them in halls, sit next to them, see them again in the coffeeshop. Then there are the special interest groups—sports, sciences, computers, language clubs, newspapers, arts—that abound on campuses. An important part of the college experience, these are places where you are likely to meet people of your particular interests. Finally of course there are the student lounges, mixers, concerts and the like where people meet people.

Candor, Authenticity, and Self-Disclosure

But being available doesn't mean just smiling and saying "Hello." To develop a caring network you must offer something of great value: yourself.

Have you ever tried to be really honest with people you have just met? It's an amazing experience. Most people aren't ready for that. It's almost frightening for them. So when I say you must be honest, I don't mean you have to be *totally* honest and brutally frank. That would be almost too weird. On the other hand, trying to make *too* good an impression is obvious and puts people off. Giving people a little bit of what they expect makes them like you. Trying too hard to be what you are not makes you a phony, and that reputation is the kiss of death. There is a fine line you mustn't cross. It is best to err on the side of authenticity, so that who you are is what you are offering, no more nor less. You must therefore learn candor, authenticity, and open self-disclosure; nothing less will do. You must be reasonably honest from the first encounter.

You're Looking Good

It is natural to want to "look good." Since we all want approval and respect, we tend to fashion an image that we think others will like. We try to project an air of confidence and competence. Indeed, confidence and competence are important, and important to project, and by behaving confidently, we become more confident. Besides, no one wants to be seen by other students as unsophisticated, unknowledgeable, and not with it. You may feel totally lost, confused, incompetent, inadequate, and a social boor. You don't know what to do next, and have forgotten your first assignment. You want to hide under the bed. Instead you smile and practice looking carefree and relaxed. Great, you're establishing a great college personality. But carried too far, this can be really dangerous for a number of reasons. The problem is, you may be doing too much damage to the real you if you bend yourself out of shape too much to please others.

If you hide your real feeling and thoughts, you are giving yourself a subtle message that it may be because your feelings and thoughts—and you—are not really worthwhile. Maybe not so subtle even; you may begin to suspect that behind your flashing smile is a pretty sleazy person. Then what approval you do get won't mean much to you because it will only be for your smiling image. If people knew what you were really like, they might cross the street when they saw you coming.

You cannot really take in and enjoy the good things that will come your way if it is only for your image. You must put any false images aside to be able to take in the approval of others. Sooner or later you have to take a chance and reveal your real self to someone if you are to feel good about yourself.

Will people like you anyway? Will you feel valued for who you really are? Who knows until you try it?

Shyness

Shyness is a terrible feeling that afflicts many, many people. If you are shy, you are not alone. Fortunately, it is usually self-limited; that is, most shy people get over it with time and good experiences. While you have it however, it can be a devastating feeling, that can lead to loneliness and isolation.

Most shy people I know are very nice, gentle, good people. When they let others get to know them, they are almost universally liked. But it is hard for others to get to know them; they are often seen by others (mistakenly) as stand-offish and conceited. It is a terrible bind for shy people.

I will talk more about shyness throughout the book, and especially in the chapter on assertiveness. For now, concentrate on reassuring yourself that although you are shy, you may actually be a very nice person whom people would really like, if you could let them know you.

What Groups Should You Join?

What groups do *you* want to join?

People tend to identify themselves with their groups. Just for a start, you will identify yourself with your family, your college, your country, your religion, your ethnic group, and any other group of which you feel a part. Your pride in your group is an important part of your feelings of self-worth.

You will probably be most comfortable, at least at first, with people who are most like you, who see the world the way you do. Mutual admiration societies make excellent support groups.

But college is an opportunity to meet people who will be different from anyone you ever met before. There are more people out there who are not like you than who are like you. You will have the opportunity to meet some of them. We all grow up with a tendency to believe that our group is the right way to be, and that there is something subtly wrong with other groups. Discovering that you may have unsuspected prejudices is one of the profoundly broadening experiences that college offers. It is sometimes something of a shock to find that what you thought you knew about some groups of people may not have been at all true. You owe it to yourself, and to society, to know as many different people as you can, and to see what conclusions you come to about this world of ours. Some of its inhabitants who you thought of as weird last year may become your best friends. So don't limit yourself.

In college and in life, there are certain groups that seem to have a certain aura, and appear to have more prestige and more worth; for example, the "Greeks." Naturally, you might want to be a part of these groups, and so share in the feeling of worth. If they represent genuine interests of yours, go for it. But if it is *only* the prestige that recommends them to you, think twice. If their interests and goals are different from yours, you will not be happy with them.

Social Acceptance

For many young people, social acceptance is an important goal on first coming into college. It is important, however, to place this goal in perspective.

Al was good-looking, had a cheerful disposition, told good jokes, chug-a-lugged a glass of beer without difficulty, and drove a Trans-Am. He was snapped up by one of the better fraternities, and embarked on a satisfying and successful social life, which included partying almost every night. Although he did not excel in his studies, he passed everything, and by the time he graduated he could chug-a-lug a quart of beer. Following graduation he found a position in a plant run by a business acquaintance of his father's, and joined a better country club.

Social competence is important in life. It is pleasant and satisfying to be part of some social group, and it can provide useful connections for a career. However, for some, social success becomes a *major* goal in college. It stops being a developmental task, a pleasant diversion, a way of making good relationships, and becomes the image, the reality, of life itself.

In some schools and some careers "connections" seem to be the name of the game. If, in your selected career, an "old boy" network is important, then play the game. But do not mistake the game for life itself. It is *not* life itself, unless you make it so. If you do, it may be all that life will be for you. It is better if socializing remains an enjoyable and even important part, but not the only or even major part, of college life. Competence and good work habits will always be integral components of success.

Have fun in college, but don't major in socializing.

Not Everyone Will Like You

Inevitably, some people will not like you. That will always hurt, and you will wonder why, and perhaps never know. Also, there will always be people who are critical of you and think you should not be the way you are. Some will be downright hostile. You must learn to handle these people and not take in their negative statements and rejections. Some tools for handling such people are in chapter 5.

It is important to accept that you cannot please everyone. Do you really want to waste your time at college trying to be friends with people who don't respect you for who you are? If you try to please everyone, you will end up pleasing no one.

The Groucho Marx Club

If you grew up being corrected and criticized, you may actually feel comfortable with criticism and with critical people. You may even think there is something wrong with people who accept and like you. It would be so much easier if we could choose as our models those people who truly value us, but we tend to join Groucho Marx's club instead.

You do remember who Groucho was, don't you? Grouch once said, "I wouldn't belong to any club that would have me as a member." Funny, and not so funny, because it touches a nerve in all of us. We all have set standards for ourselves that most of us cannot reach.

In the meantime, it is much easier and more rewarding to make friends with those who approve of and like you. You will have to do some experimenting to find out for yourself how much, and with whom, openness is advisable.

The problem then is to find friends with whom to share your thoughts, feelings and concerns, and from whom you will in return receive support, validation, and understanding.

Your First Love Affair
At College

Your first love affair at college is likely to be compelling. It is likely to have elements of everything we have discussed so far, and more. It will include love, of course, and sex. But it will also include strong feelings of caring, and being cared for, and so will arouse dependency needs, and also the need for independence. Your child will come out to play, and you will feel responsible and adult. You will feel needy and will receive; you will be selfless and giving.

It may be an ideal relationship, one in which you feel a great deal of support when you need it, and space when you need that. The other person will "be there" for you when you have need, and will not intrude when you need to be alone. He or she will be accepting of you, under-standing, and caring, and you of him or her.

But at this stage in your life, it is more likely that both of you will have too many conflicts about dependency and independency, closeness and rejection. You will have too many issues still to resolve, issues of commitment, respon-sibility, and the exploration of other relationships. You are still testing your limits and those of others. You will experience hurt, disappointment, anger, self-doubt, and insecurity. At this stage in your life, you are still working on too many problems associated with growing up, and your first affair may not survive.

I will talk more about handling the pain and depression you may experience, in Chapter 12. Separating from this relationship may be one of the most painful things you will ever do.

Separation Anxiety

The fear that we might lose a relationship sometimes makes us clutch it so tightly we strangle it to death. The more insecure and anxious we are about others, the tighter we hold them. This can make our relationships confusing and awkward.

Separation anxiety occurs when we have fears related to our being nurtured. Nurturing is an important part of living, necessary for life itself. It is a basic need of all people.

Ordinarily, we are not too concerned about nurturing. If, as children, we got enough of it, we felt loved and worthwhile and safe and secure in our relationships. We knew we were all right.

A famous English psychiatrist, John Bowlby,* described the behavior of a two-year-old boy with his mother in a park. At first the child hangs onto her skirt. After a while he lets go, and starts exploring. He comes back and holds on a little longer, then he goes off again, further. After a short time, he ignores her completely, and plays happily with the other children.

You can understand how a child who is not sure of his mother's love will hang on to her skirts and find it hard to move away. He will have "separation anxiety."

If we have a great deal of anxiety about our relationship with another person, then we must look to our basic sense of nurturing. If anybody is capable of making us feel anxious because they might leave us, we must realize that it is because we suspect we are not worthwhile enough to be cared for and caring.

We may realistically fear another will leave us. We become anxious only if it threatens our own basic need to be nurtured.

If you can learn to deal with this anxiety, you can relate better to others and enjoy them more. The paradox is that to form close and lasting relationships, you must be able to let go of them if necessary.

EXERCISE 1. Separation and Grief

Purpose: To learn to deal with the feelings caused by separation.

Method: Think about a person with whom you have

Attachment and Loss (New York: Basic Books, 1969).

or have had a close relationship. This exercise does not mean that you have to end the relationship, only that you would be able to if the need to do so arose. Start by describing the parts of the person that you admire and value, that you would like for yourself, or that you would be willing to take into yourself. Remember the good feelings you have had together. Then, when you are re-experiencing these good feelings, do something physical. Psychologists Richard Bandler and John Grinder simply touch the person who is having these feelings on the knee, or the arm; later, touching them again in the same place brings forth the same feelings. It almost seems like magic. In fact, they called their first book, *The Structure of Magic.* * You can do this for yourself by gently pressing your arm with your hand. In this way, thoughts of the other person will call forth good feelings, and you will have internalized that person as your approving other.

Sometimes, as part of grief, feelings of anger, guilt, or resentment may be present. You may even be angry at the other person for leaving you. It is important to express and to accept these negative feelings as natural and normal. Blocking them ("I shouldn't feel this way!") will block your other good feelings.

Finally, practice saying goodbye. Out loud. Sometimes just saying the words, "Goodbye, (name)" can cause intense feelings to well up. You must allow this! Suppressing these feelings makes them go underground and persist. It may take weeks, but if every once in a while you say, "Goodbye, (name)," the painful edge of the grief will become eased much sooner.

Comment: The loss of a relationship always leaves a

* (Palo Alto, Ca.: Science and Behavior Books, 1976)*

hole, like a cigarette burn in a fabric. It is important to start reweaving that fabric. You do this by talking about the person, and the value that the person had for you; and as you do so, let the people you are telling this to supply some of what you have lost. But if your dependency needs were involved, you may have a hard time facing up to the fact that, after childhood, being taken care of by another person is, and always will be, an illusion.

Nurturing Yourself

Periods of time will inevitably occur in your life when you are between caring relationships or when these relationships do not meet your emotional needs. It is at times like these that you have the opportunity to learn how to take good care of yourself and your inner child. You can learn to nurture yourself.

A word about that inner child of yours. Everyone has one. Even you. Part of the stress of young adulthood is the fact that your childhood was so recent and you may have such a strong desire to be mature that you disown and deny your inner child. But it is really important to acknowledge and cherish that part of you. Unrestrained, of course, it can cause you considerable mischief, but it is also the source of much joy and pleasure. If you repress it, you will become boring and even depressed.

The following exercise will acknowledge this child in you. As you read the exercise you may have some difficulty. The feelings associated with having an inner child may be so uncomfortable that you may not want to deal with them and so may deny them and try to escape. But if you allow yourself to do this exercise, I promise you it will be a good experience.

EXERCISE 2. Your Inner Child

Purpose: To recognize and cope with your own "inner child."

Method: Picture your inner child as a smaller edition of yourself. Do you know a small child? Imagine what it would feel like to have such a child inside you, completely irresponsible, happy, demanding, unhappy.

Sit in a chair, and fantasize this "child" sitting on your lap. If this is too hard for you, it may be easier to imagine this "child" sitting in another chair. Listen carefully to your child tell you what it wants and needs. Then, as the adult you, affirm your child, explain the situation, and reassure it that it will be taken care of, by you. See if you can sustain a short conversation.

Comment: By getting in touch with the feelings of your inner child, who wants to be taken care of, you can then get in touch with your "adult," who will decide what is best for the two of you. It is up to you, the adult, to make the final executive decisions. Letting your inner child make your decisions in crucial situations can be dangerous. When you are dealing with life, let your adult side do the negotiating.

Growing up means that you are now able to take charge of your own needs so that you will not have to blame others when those needs are not met.

Face it. The only one who can really take care of you, is you.

2 Let's Talk about Sex

Jacqueline Kansky*

o you feel awkward and worried when you consider having sex?

Sex is a natural function of the body. Male babies are often born with erections, and in sleep men have erections and women lubricate every ninety

* Jacqueline Kansky is a marriage and family counselor and sex therapist practicing in Los Altos, California.

minutes. Thus, sexual response is automatic and spontaneous given favorable circumstances. So why is sex so confusing?

In our society we are taught two opposing lessons about sex: first, how to enjoy sensual feelings, and second, how to inhibit those feelings. As infants we are held, cuddled, fed, rocked, and sung to, but also, we are limited as to when, where, how, and with whom we can be sensual, warm, and close. As we mature, the sexual drive increases the urge for pleasure, and society increases its vigilance and sexual inhibitions. As young adults begin to understand both the positive and negative consequences of having sex and learn ways of having "safe-sex," they can begin to make decisions about their own sexuality. What are the consequences of having sex? The negatives are unwanted pregnancy, abortion, single parenthood, marriage for the wrong reasons, sexually transmitted diseases, and emotional disruption. But don't forget the positives!—sensual pleasure, discovery, ego-boosts from joyful, confident sex, becoming a sexual person, and that wonderful unparalleled state of being emotionally close to another human being.

So, sex is a natural function which has been restrained and inhibited. The ratio of pleasure to inhibition is unique for each person. What happens upon entering college? Students are away from external "inhibitors" and suddenly can do anything they want—free thought, free action, free love. But can they? Somewhere inside the inhibitors reside, saying the same old things: "Do this, don't do that, you'll be sorry." Along with the pressure of classes, separation from family, loneliness, and new living situations, there is the biological pressure of sex and

a new societal pressure, this time with an opposite message—have sex. There are too many lessons to learn, too
many choices, and mostly there is *confusion.*

Now is a time to find out about your personal sexual
identity. What do you like, what don't you like, what
makes you joyous, what makes you guilty? How can you
be emotionally comfortable, assess consequences, plan
healthy sex, take responsibility back from others, become
a separate, unique, sexual being?

Discovering your sexuality is a lifetime voyage; there is
no rush. The biological sexual urge, the wish for pleasure,
can be balanced by emotional comfort. Measure your
emotional comfort. If your anxiety is high, honor that.
Sex is not an emergency; it can be allowed to grow gradually as each person feels ready, from knowing your own
body, to kissing another, to petting, to comfort with nudity, to touching another sexually, to intercourse. Each
step moves toward a gradual understanding of what is
right for you, a sorting process with the attendant joy of
success. The sense of discovery need not be overwhelmed
by anxiety and fear of failure or consequence. Sex can be
healthy, safe, pleasurable, and fun.

On Becoming a Non-Virgin

How do you know when you are ready to become a
non-virgin? Be true to yourself. Ask yourself some questions.

Am I comfortable with nudity and touching? Do I feel
confident as a sexual being or do I feel confused? Do I feel
pressured by peers or a lover, or is it my own wish to have

sex? Can I prepare for safe, healthy sex? Will I like myself later?

Answers to these questions may help you decide what is right for you. A thoughtful, comfortable decision will reduce anxiety and enhance your first sexual experience.

Some students feel that virginity is such a burden that they want to have intercourse for the sole purpose of a change of state. They may have intercourse with a prostitute or an older, more experienced person, or the next person they date. The idea is to "get it over with," with someone they do not know or care about or are likely to see again. Students have described these experiences as disappointing, degrading, dehumanizing, or upsetting. The first intercourse may color your feelings about sex for a long time, so give yourself a chance, and invest some energy into making this step a positive one.

Remember that anxiety and worry can diminish the pleasure of sex, so try to create a comfortable atmosphere. Most students have their first intercourse with a partner they know. Choose a partner that you like and trust, someone who will listen and respond to you if you want something different or you are uncomfortable. Even though you are a novice, you may expect to perform like a veteran. This is unrealistic. Your first sexual experience is an adventure and a time of discovery. As you become more experienced, pleasure will increase.

Pregnancy and Abortion

An unplanned pregnancy has far-reaching effects on a couple. If they are both involved in the discovery and decision about what to do, strong emotional feelings and issues arise. Will they marry? Are they ready to become parents? Must they interrupt their studies and potential careers to have a baby? How will they tell their parents? Should they abort? Do they agree either that abortion is morally wrong for them or that abortion would be a relief and the best decision? If they disagree, what then? There are no easy answers to these questions. They will be different for each couple. Talking with each other and with a counselor will you help get through a difficult time.

Often the woman carries the burden of the decision regarding pregnancy alone. She must struggle with moral issues, with physical changes in her body, and with the potential of loss and sadness. Pregnancy forces changes. Doing nothing is a decision in itself. Early exploration of the issues allows time to be clear about what is best for you. If you decide to have an abortion, have it performed early. Each day a woman's body changes and she becomes more attached to the fetus growing within her. If it is not to be, face it, and end it. It is normal to feel sadness after an abortion, even if you are greatly relieved and comfortable with your decision.

Contraception

The responsibility for birth control is with both partners; both should be aware of what contraceptive method is being used. For young people in their first sexual encounter this is rarely the case. It has been estimated that 70 percent of 15- to 19-year-old sexually active partners are not using birth control or only use it sometimes. Many young women use birth control only after their first intercourse or pregnancy. As a result, about 17 percent of the women of this age group become pregnant. Young men also often do not take their share of responsibility for contraception. In an age when birth control is easily available, why do men and women have unprotected intercourse?

In a perfect world, one could simply say birth control is a practical and desirable practice for the sexually active person. But in our society with so many mixed messages regarding sex, confusion reigns. For the woman considering birth control, myriad issues assail her. Am I bad because I have sexual feelings and want sex? It's one thing to want sex, but far different to plan for it. Will my parents find out and judge me harshly? I know I should get birth control, but it is so embarrassing to go to the clinic or to my family doctor and ask for it. Will I need a pelvic examination? If so, I will feel so exposed and vulnerable that I may not be able to go through with it. Will I be seen entering or leaving the clinic? It is so much easier to be swept away by someone else and not be responsible for what happens.

If possible, separate the practical need for birth control and the wish for healthy sex, from the moral and emotional issues. Part of being ready for sexual activity is being ready for birth control. The decision to use birth control is a step which can resonate with a woman's independence and assertiveness. She is taking care of her own body and her own future in her own way, and not relying on a man to take care of her.

There are a number of different kinds of birth control methods. A woman can choose one suited to her own desires and her pattern of sexual activity. This is an individual, personal matter. After choosing a method, the next challenge is to use it as prescribed, consistently and effectively.

It is the man's responsibility to know what method of contraception the woman is using, and in addition to use a condom. The condom provides a "barrier" method which not only serves as a birth control method, but decreases the chance of spreading sexually transmitted diseases. Both the man and women should make sure that it is available and used. The woman should consider that a man who does not ask about her contraceptive method or who does not carry a condom, would not make a reliable partner. Condoms are readily available and their use enjoys wide acceptance. Men have fewer emotional problems with the use of contraception than do women. Again, follow directions carefully and consistently for best results.

Dysfunctions

"I'm afraid something will go wrong . . ."

We have seen that sex is a natural function, and that given positive, erotic circumstances all systems will "work." Erections for men and vaginal lubrication for women cannot be willed to happen or forced, but appear spontaneously in response to sexual excitement and atmosphere. You may be surprised to know that the most important sexual organ is the *brain.* The brain responds to sights, smells, sounds, and touch with sexual pleasure, and becomes excited and joyful. The pleasure centers are in the brain. But the brain is also the inhibitor, the worrier, the hurrier, the judge, and the critical downgrader.

When something goes wrong sexually, most of the time

the origin of the trouble is in the mind. Three conditions which may interfere with the mood and with easy exploration of sex are the 3 A's: Anxiety, Anger, and Alcohol. For college students, the most important factor interfering with sexual pleasure and effectiveness is anxiety or worry.

Men worry about ejaculating too soon, being embarrassed, and feeling inadequate. When primitive man mated, he was vulnerable to predators so that rapid ejaculation was a matter of survival. It is not abnormal to ejaculate quickly. In today's culture, the ability to prolong intercourse enhances the pleasure of both men and women. Learning to "last longer" is an acquired skill—it takes practice. After a period of abstinence, men tend to ejaculate more quickly than when they have regular sex. Fear of being discovered, or a female partner who doesn't like sex and wants to get sex over in a hurry (or prostitutes who want to get their customers in and out as fast as possible), can contribute to forming a pattern of rapid ejaculation. Establishing a leisurely pace with adequate privacy and concentration on pleasurable sensations, may help prolong sex.

Another problem for men is the inability to get an erection when they want one. This condition is often caused by anxiety or by excessive use of alcohol. Rarely is something physically wrong with the sexual organs. Here again the brain has its say. It tells us, "The more worry, the less performance." The more a man fears he won't achieve an erection, the more he tries to will one to appear, the more he monitors, checks, and watches for results, the less response he will get from his sexual organ. So what is the key? Relax, be aware of and enjoy all the sexual feelings, and be assured that your automatically sexual, functional body will respond. Take the mental pressures away and your body will do the rest. Trust your-self.

The effects of alcohol consumption are more complicated. Small amounts of alcohol loosen moral, sexual inhibitions in the brain and thus may allow the body to respond more readily. Larger amounts, however, may reduce the physical response of the body, particularly the spontaneous appearance of an erection. Alcohol increases sexual desire and reduces sexual response.

Women may also be worried, but for them the effects are different. Their sexual response is hidden, not open to scrutiny and judgment, so they are less concerned with performance than men are. They can play-act and get away with it. Anxiety, however, may reduce lubrication so that intercourse becomes uncomfortable or even painful. "Vaginismus" is an automatic spasm, much like a cramp, when something is introduced into the vagina, and can be painful. This can be treated, so don't tough it out. See a physician. Sex does not need to be painful; give it a chance.

Women are also concerned about orgasm. They may have certain expectations and be disappointed by their sexual experience. The art of arousal and the enhancement of sexual feelings develops more slowly than in men. Women reach their peak of sexuality in their late thirties. The normal pattern is a slow, protracted appreciation of sexuality. Orgasm is learned, both by loosening inhibitions and by becoming more and more aware of the kinds of touch, movements and situations that work best for each individual woman. Each woman is unique, and discovery of her potential includes a discovery of her sexual self.

Sexually Transmitted Diseases

Unfortunately, sexually transmitted diseases (STDs) are a fact of life in today's social/sexual scene. The century-old diseases gonorrhea and syphilis are still here, but have been upstaged by more contemporary conditions like herpes, venereal warts, and chlamydia, infections which are of epidemic proportions today. Most recently the seriousness of Acquired Immune Deficiency Syndrome (AIDS) and the less severe AIDS Related Diseases (ARD) have begun to alter sexual patterns. Although certain groups of people are considered "at risk" for AIDS and ARDs (gay men, drug users, and hemophiliacs) the possibility of infection exists in heterosexual men and women.

For some students the fear of disease precludes the pleasure of sex. Others prefer not to think about infection at all ("If I don't think about it it doesn't exist"). How can students practice safe sex and reduce the probability of infection? Avoidance of the issue is the most dangerous course. Several actions may help, however. First, take the mystery out of STDs—be informed. Second, use a condom or ask your partner to use one. This "barrier" method is not 100 percent effective, but greatly reduces the chance of infection. Third, reduce the number of sexual partners, and fourth, know your partner. Ask about and look for signs of infection in yourself and others. Have any lesions checked by a physician as soon as possible. Immediate treatment is important to avoid long-term effects.

Sexual Orientation

Sexual orientation, whether a person is homosexual or heterosexual, is of concern to both sexes, but more to men than to women. It has been estimated that 30 percent of college men have had some homosexual contact. This does not necessarily mean they are gay; the atmosphere of experimentation at college brings some pressure on students to have various sexual experiences.

What is homosexuality? A homosexual/gay person is one who prefers having sex with another person of the same sex. It is also a way of life; there is a gay culture which has many positive attributes. There are many false myths about homosexuality. It is not immoral, it is not a mental illness, and it is not "learned." Gay people know they are gay often from a very early age. Like any minority group, gay people must assert themselves to avoid either self-blame or discrimination.

College men have many concerns about their masculinity, and whether or not they are "normal." If a male student is a virgin or doesn't like oral sex, one-night stands, sports, has a sexual dysfunction, feels close to another male student or is shy, he may fear he is gay. None of the above conditions, by themselves, make a homosexual.

Women also have concerns about their feminity and sexual orientation. Women are in general taught to be more "caring" and sensual than men. As girls, they hug, kiss, touch and get touched more than boys. They "practice" their sensuality with each other without insecurity or embarrassment, in a spirit of playfulness and experimentation, and in so doing create strong bonds with each other.

In addition, the women's movement has produced an attitude of independence, and also of isolation from men. In this atmosphere, somewhat like that of an all female boarding school, there may be more confusion regarding choice of sexual partners than in the past.

If you feel confused about your sexual orientation, talk to a professional who can help you sort out your thoughts and feelings. Uncertainty about sexual orientation can be a disturbing issue for many students.

Casual Sex

Students have mixed feelings about casual sex. The idea of having sex with different partners for the physical experience alone is intriguing. No attachment, no emotional involvement, just pure sex. Many students equate casual sex with freedom and feel that if they were really liberated they would like casual sex. If they are not comfortable with this kind of sexuality, they wonder if they are too rigid or square. The number of young adults who enjoy random, uncommitted intercourse is probably small. There is still a lot of tradition, love, and romance associated with sex. The binding of tenderness toward another person with erotic feelings changes the physical experience. As this bond strengthens, intimacy, with either short- or long-term commitment, may follow. There is no "normal" degree of casual sex or committed sex. Each person searches for what is right for him/her at this time of his/her life.

3 Listening

The most important part of making a good relationship is listening to others. With all the talking that people do, it seems strange to me that no one really learns how to listen. I remember being told that it is important to be a good listener, but no one ever explained to me what that really meant. For some students, the hour they spend learning how to listen can bring a new approach to life. They say, "Until now, I thought people just listened!"

Most people in this world don't really listen to you. They may hear your words, but they don't give you their full attention. Often they are just waiting until your voice stops so that they can tell you what is on their mind. Sometimes they don't even wait.

For most people, conversation is played like a game of Trivial Pursuit; each person competes to see who goes next with the best piece of information. It is no wonder that the game itself became so popular; it gave formal expression to the way people talk anyway. I don't want to run this type of conversation down; it has a definite place. But if that is all there is, it places relationships on a trivial level.

If you have felt lonely and dissatisfied in a roomful of chattering people, it is probably because you have been competing in an informal game of Trivia. Even when everyone else seems to be having fun, you may be wishing there were better ways of relating to people. If you too have been guilty of trivializing your relationships, you may wish to learn a more effective way of making friends.

I Thought People Just Talked

On the other hand, you may have some resistance to learning "a more effective way of making friends." It sounds as if it might be insincere, manipulative, phony. Of course you want to make friends, but you want to have it happen naturally. You don't want rules to follow. You want to be who you are, and to have people either like you or not, and to be honest about it. You probably know people who listen and pretend to like you just so you will like them, and you really don't like them, and you don't want to be like that.

Of course I understand that, and I agree. But I am not talking about pretending or about getting people to like you. I am talking about something different. I am talking about empathic listening, giving people your full listening attention so that you understand them better. This is for your benefit, not theirs. It allows you to hear what they are really saying, and to find out what they are really like. It gives you the choice of knowing people before you decide whether you like them or not. It lets you explore how other people see the world, and gives you better options. It allows you to avoid quick, superficial impressions. It helps you.

It may be that you will be also be a more likable person. But that is not why you listen empathetically.

Learning how to listen empathetically does have certain general rules, but they are flexible, and once you understand the process, you can abandon the rules. You might think empathic listening should occur naturally, but it often does not. If you are not used to it, it may even seem awkward at first, and will take courage to try, and practice to get used to, like any skill. A little courage, and a lot of practice.

If you are interested in empathic listening, start just by listening and paying attention to other students. For the next few days, I would like you to listen carefully to conversations, even while you are taking part in them. You might notice that there are three general levels of conversation.

The Trivia Contest

1. As I said, the trivia contest is most common. Here we spend our time telling others about things, events, sports, teachers, incidents, what happened last night, who did what with whom, who said what. That's O.K.; it is fun, and an important part of socialization and life. But it is not the stuff of which the more satisfying relationships are made.

The Bull Session

2. The bull session is a slightly deeper level of relating. Here we get interested in what it all *means!* We talk about world happenings and the cosmic significance of events. We explain and argue about philosophy, politics, religion, and the meaning of life. Deep stuff, intellectually stimulating, and an important part of life. But again, we leave without feeling that we have made real contact.

Sharing Thoughts and Feelings

3. Sharing thoughts and feelings is the most difficult level, but the level at which relationships are cemented. It is the level at which people share their thoughts about *themselves* and *each other,* and their *feelings* about what is happening. At the usual lunchroom or brief, between classes encounters, this level would probably be inappropriate. It needs a quiet place and a receptive person. It is the most satisfying level of conversation, and the one in which we are most apt to become tongue-tied, and awkward.

Ways of Listening

At each of these levels, I want you to practice

> *mirroring*
> *listening for free information*
> *affirming*
> *self-disclosure*

in that order.

These are new terms for you, I'm sure. As I said, no one teaches much about how to listen. I guarantee that *these* assignments will be fun, and will lead to good things.

Mirroring

Mirroring is a way of letting your body and your facial expressions adopt the posture and movements and expressions of another person, just for a moment, *without being obvious* about it. If you have never done this, try it the very next time you see anyone. You may be surprised to find that by adopting the other person's physical movements and expression, you get a set of feelings and even beliefs that you know did not come from you. There is such a close relationship between the way people feel or how they see the world, and the way they look and move, that by copying the latter, you experience the former. In a sense, you get under their skin and, for a short time, become that person. You get to know the other person very well, very quickly.

You may also be surprised to find that the other person will *not* notice what you are doing, but will just relax and become more comfortable with you. If they do notice, you have been too obvious about it. It really just takes the slightest of movements, the hint of a facial expression. It's the internal feel of your muscles you want to experience. After you get over the strangeness of mirroring, you will become more comfortable with other people, because you will know them better, and know what to expect.

Free Information

In addition, listen for *free information.* Free information is information that in some way does not relate to what has been said or asked. Free information is something that the other person is willing to talk about, perhaps even *wants* to talk about, but only if you ask. It is something just on the fringes of their minds, something thrown out in passing. If, for example, you are talking about a new concept from your philosophy 101 class, and the other person mentions the philosophy of suicide, you can later bring up the subject of suicide and probably hear a great deal you did not expect. It depends somewhat on how irrelevant the free information is to what you were discussing; the more irrelevant the more likely to be important to the other person. You then know that you can bring up that subject at any time and the other person will have something to say about it.

You might think that it is impolite to ask about something that was brought up so indirectly and tangentially. But such free information is a trial balloon, sent up to test the climate. If you respond to it, you will reassure the other person that it is all right to say more about that subject.

Affirming

Affirming means to listen carefully to what the other person says, and then to let him/her know, in a positive way, that you have indeed heard what was said, and that you find it worthwhile.

How do you do this? First, you must not only listen carefully and attentively, you must let the other person *know* that you are listening. Don't just assume that they know. Keep glancing at the other person's eyes, lean forward a little, show your interest.

Second, you must show the other person by your words and actions that you have actually understood. You do this by occasionally nodding your head, and saying "Yeah," or some such similar phrase. Then you may repeat a key word or phrase of theirs, or even rephrase a whole thought, and look to see if you got it right.

If you are not used to affirming others, it can be harder to do than you might think. It may feel more natural just to go ahead with your response, or your own ideas. But people really like something more affirmative.

"It's better to live off campus; you have more independence."

"That's true, but it is so much easier to meet people on campus."

"Sure it is, but you only need a few good friends."

"Yes, and I like being one of them. It's just that I feel better when I have a lot of people around me."

Look how different it is, when the affirming "That's true," "Sure," and "Yes" is left out.

"It's better to live off campus; you have more independence."

"It's easier to meet people on campus."

"But you only need a few good friends."

"Well, I like a lot of people around me."

The first two pairs of people are sharing their thoughts, and will like other. The last two may not know any way to relate to others except by arguing. Without really intending to, they are playing "I'll tell you why you are wrong and I'm right." At its best, it is an interesting intellectual exercise. At its worst it is a "who's smarter, who's stupider" competition. In such a "conversation" both lose. Have *you* ever participated in a conversation where the other person never really acknowledged what you said? It doesn't feel very good.

Affirming another person does not mean that you necessarily agree, only that you have heard and understood. You are then free to disagree, if you wish. If you do disagree, affirming the other person first avoids the common difficulty, that the other person believes you disagree only because you didn't really understand. He then spends a lot of time and energy saying the same thing in different ways, hoping that if he says it loud enough you will finally hear and agree.

Self-Disclosure

When you have affirmed the other person, and not until then, *share your own thoughts* that relate in some way to what the other person was saying. Stay, at least for a while, on the same level of conversation as the other person. If the subject is trivia, stay on trivia, and if the subject is feelings, then share your feelings.

Appropriate self-disclosure is itself a powerful stimulus to further conversation and to self-disclosure by the other person. Conversations run on the fuel of new information now and then. How much self-disclosure is appropriate depends on the circumstances. A monologue about yourself is never appropriate, and no self-disclosure at all will ordinarily turn off a conversation, so that it dies a painful death. In fact, if you want not to talk to someone, just don't volunteer any information, and the other person will soon break off contact.

These four actions, of getting a feel for another person by mirroring, listening carefully for "free information," affirming that person's thoughts or feelings, and then sharing your own thoughts or feelings, are powerful in forming an atmosphere in which relationships can flourish.

Changing the Level of Conversation

There are a few other things to keep in mind. For example, it is quite disconcerting to have the level of conversation suddenly deepened. If the subject is rent and you express your feelings about loneliness, you may find yourself ignored. Many people are not willing to pick up on these things. The reverse is also true; it is disconcerting to suddenly make the level more superficial. If the subject is the other person's feelings, and you respond with a bit of clever philosophy, you may kill a budding relationship. Of course, if that is what you want to do, it works quite well.

When you do want to change the subject or the level, do so, but with a transition statement, and keep an eye on the reaction you get. Send up a trial balloon and see what happens. Others may or may not be willing to listen to your feelings, and it does no good to talk when you don't have an audience. If you don't get a response, drop it. You may have misjudged the situation. The circumstances may be wrong or the person not open to you. Try another time or another person.

Questions

A good way to begin a conversation is with an *open-ended question.* An open-ended question is one that cannot be answered by "Yes" or "No." For example you might say, "What did you think of that lecture?" rather than, "Did you like that lecture?" Or, "Who are all these people?" rather than "Do you know any of the people here?" You can even get by with "What's happening?" The answer will tell you a lot; a monosyllabic answer to an open-ended question is a good clue not to waste your time.

But beware of asking too many questions. A few questions show interest, but too many questions become an interrogation. They may produce a conversation of sorts, but generally one that becomes uncomfortable. Too many questions do nothing to promote a relationship.

Being Right

You may have strong ideas on various matters. It may be hard to learn that you get will not win relationship points for being right or clever outside of class. In fact, it is almost a sure way of getting people to sit somewhere else.

And while you are sharing your thoughts, never, never put down the ideas or feelings of others. If you turn out to be wrong, you will look foolish. It is even worse if you are right, and the other person feels foolish..You may win the argument, but they may never forgive you. Of course, you must decide for yourself whether or not the relationship is more important for you than the idea.

To become comfortable with these ideas may take much practice. The next exercise will help you summarize and practice them.

EXERCISE 3. Reflecting

In the dining room (or anywhere else appropriate), sit down near someone you don't know. Ask the other person an open-ended question about anything that seems appropriate; for example, some current campus concern. Go through the following steps, in order:

1. When you first sit down, nod, smile, and internally mirror the other person's posture and expression. Then ask your open-ended question.

2. Listen *silently* to the reply until the person has finished, and then make an affirmative response. Reflect a few *key words* of the last sentence.

3. If the other person then continues, wait for the next break, and then reflect the *sense* of what was said; *paraphrase the thought or belief.* In addition, try to gain a sense of the *feeling* that is underlying the statements, and then check this out, say what that feeling is, and see if that is really what the other person is feeling.

4. Then share with the other person some experience of your *own* that made you feel something of what the other person is feeling.

Comment: For the purpose of this exercise, avoid criticism, competition, or giving advice. Keep on the positive and affirming side.

———————

This may feel awkward at first, and not "you." The more awkward it seems, however, the more important this exercise may be for you. When you are comfortable with it, try it with someone you know. If you have a good response and a good experience, the feeling of awkwardness will quickly pass.

4 Self-Awareness

Charlie's father is a very successful physician. Charlie didn't see too much of him when he was growing up, but he loved and respected him, and wanted to follow in his footsteps.

He did well at all his studies except biology and biochemistry. As hard as he tried, he just couldn't "get it." One day, his chem teacher said to him, "Charlie, maybe you don't really *want* to go to medical school."

"Of course I do," he insisted indignantly. "I've always wanted to go to medical school."

"Well, maybe on one level you do want to go, and maybe on another level there is a part of you that doesn't want to go. Is there anything else you would like to do?"

As it happens, Charlie sang very well, and spent a lot of his time in clubs, listening to the performers. He had even had a few successful gigs of his own at a local club.

"Of course it's foolish, but I would enjoy show business. I do some singing. But that's no career."

"Maybe you should take some time and think it over."

"My father would just die!"

You never know. Charlie's father didn't die. He supported his son in his decision, and even boasted to friends about his son, the singer. About three years later, he stopped performing, and became a representative for other artists. Now, he makes more money than his father, and, what is more important, is enjoying his life. Of course, he has problems, but they are his problems, not his father's.

Who Are You?

In some ways, you are like other people; for example, you probably share a need for nurturing, and you inherited some characteristics from your family, who you probably resemble (you may be the spitting image of your mother's grandfather). On the other hand, you are certainly different from any of the billions of other people who live, or who have ever lived, on this planet. Your genetic makeup is different from any other individual. Even if you are an identical twin, you have had experiences no one else has had, and when you have shared experiences with others, you saw them differently and came to different conclusions.

You are unique. But who are you, really?

The following few exercises may help you develop a heightened sense of who you are.

EXERCISE 4. Identity

Purpose: To develop self-awareness.

Method: Take a stack of blank 3 by 5 cards and on each write one answer to the question, "Who am I?" You may wish to include your important roles and relationships, your goals, your various needs, the things you do and don't value about yourself, or your important beliefs and behaviors.

Arrange the cards in the order of their relative importance to you, and how you see yourself as a person. Number them in order. When you are through, discard them, one at a time, starting with the least important. Look at each card carefully, and think about how it would feel not to have that part of you. When they are all gone, you may have a strange, empty feeling. Replace the half dozen most important to you. How does that feel?

Next, on a large piece of paper, at least twelve inches across, draw a circle within a circle, like a doughnut. Divide the doughnut into six parts. Now look at the cards you kept. In each section of your doughnut, draw a symbol, with colored pencils, felt-tipped pens, or soft pastels, that represents that part of you. For example, if you had "swimmer" on one of the cards, draw a symbol that will represent what "swimmer" means to you. Perhaps some waves, or just a blue color.

Color the central core and print your name in it. Tack this symbolic picture of yourself on your bathroom mirror, and look at it now and then to remind yourself of who you really are.

Comment: It is the nature of life that we get pulled in different directions, sometimes one way, sometimes another. Often people have standards that are different from yours, and think you should be more like them. Sometimes people expect things from you, that may not be right for you. You will deal better with the expectations of others if you take a good look at yourself now and then. It will help you steer a straighter course.

Comparing Differences

We have a tendency to compare ourselves with other people, and to "put down" the ways in which we are different. I knew a beautiful young woman who cringed just because her feet were larger than most women's.

But also we define ourselves by the ways in which we are different from others. We need to respect our own uniqueness. To emphasize this, we may go to extremes just to be different, even to the extent of being weird. This gives you the best of both worlds: you show how different you are from the "others," and you have an "in" group, who finds pleasures in their common condition. At the moment, colored hair is "in"; however, this probably means that it will soon be, or is already, "out." When too many people adopt a "different" style, it becomes the norm against which the next reaction must take place.

This conflict, of wanting to be similar and different at the same time, would not be so severe if we could accept how different we really are. If we were comfortable with being different, it would not be an issue.

The following exercise may help accept that you are already a unique and different human being, and that being different is both remarkable and usual.

EXERCISE 5. Comparing Differences

Purpose: To enjoy being different.

Method: Sit down with a friend and take turns mentioning ways in which you are different from each other. Don't evaluate the difference, that is, don't talk about which is better or worse, just keep looking for differences until you cannot think of any more. Explore physical differences, social differences, and psychological differences. Be aware of your feelings as you admit being different, and the feelings you have toward the other person as that person reveals differences.

Comment: At first you may feel some embarrassment about being different, but as you continue this exercise, that feeling is likely to be replaced by one of pride in your uniqueness. This process, of sharing areas of difference and watching the embarrassment subside, is an important process for you. It leads to a much better feeling about yourself and good feelings about your friend that may include relief, trust, and affection. Acknowledging your true nature to yourself and others, is likely to lead to the revelation that your unique nature is human and rather nice. Even when distressing to you. "I have acne" will probably give permission to your partner to say, "And I have big ears, and *they* won't go away." As a side product, you may not have to proclaim and flaunt your differences if you are really comfortable with them. Furthermore, the similarities that remain are just as important as your individuality; good relationships need and are built on both.

What Is Your Jungian Type?

Another way of defining the similarities and differences between you and other people is to take some version of the Jungian Types test. Jung was a Swiss psychoanalyst who described three different pairs of viewpoints from which people see the world. Each viewpoint in the pair is opposite the other, at the ends of a continuum. No one is really all the way out at either end, but we are all weighted one way or the other (see Appendix B).

Katherine Briggs and her daughter, Isabel Myers, although not themselves psychologists, were interested in Jung's description of types of personality, and created a test (the Myers-Briggs test) based on his descriptions. This test has been given to many thousands of people in all walks of life, with some interesting results.

Introversion and Extroversion

Jung noticed, for example, and Briggs and Myers have confirmed, that there are people who are more self-motivated than others. They do their thinking by themselves, study by themselves, and decide what things mean, and what they want to do, by themselves. Not entirely, of course, but more so; it is a tendency. He called this tendency in people, introversion (turned inward). Therefore introverts are less influenced by and socialize less with other people. Introverts seem to get their energy to do things, and their thoughts, mostly from inside themselves.

Extroverts on the other hand get energy and ideas from others, and are much more sociable and gregarious. When they run out of energy, they reach for the phone—they need people to charge them up. Extroverts enjoy groups more. They work better, study better, and play better in a group.

Briggs and Myers documented that there are more extroverts than introverts in our culture. As a nation we have extrovert values, so that in general, extroverts are more admired and valued. Extroverts don't understand introverts very well, and mistakenly often see them as shy, withdrawn, unsociable and unfriendly. However they envy introverts their self-reliance and independence, and say about them, "Still waters run deep!"

For their part, introverts envy the social ease and good relationships of extroverts, but see them as shallow and too easily influenced by others. In addition, both are apt at times to put *themselves* down for characteristics that are really perfectly all right and natural for them.

Not only do you have to deal with the negative perceptions of the opposite type, but you have to deal with your own negative perceptions of yourself. Introverts have to understand that being an introvert, with its own special values and pleasures, is just as good, and in many ways better, than being an extrovert, and that you would not change places with extroverts, even if you could. And extroverts must also accept the pleasures and benefits of extroversion without putting themselves down for not being like their more self-motivated friends. And as I said earlier, *self-acceptance is the key to change;* when you have really accepted who you are, you may begin to change; then extreme introverts may become more social, and extreme extroverts may become more self-reliant.

Sensates and Intuitives

Jung also described sensation and intuition as the two ends of another continuum. (You may remember that he wrote in German, and these translations do not exactly match our usual use of these words.)

He said that sensates are the realists, who tend to enjoy the practical, down to earth aspects of life. They define reality in terms of what they can see and touch. They are sensible, careful and systematic. They pay attention to detail, and like the "tried and true" ways of doing things. They are not innovators, but they are good at carrying out specific assignments. They make great executive vice-presidents.

On the other hand, intuitives pay more attention to symbolic, artistic, and spiritual values. They are the dreamers and innovators. They search for the meaning behind the obvious, and see possibilities and patterns that are invisible to others. They read between the lines. They like frequent new challenges and get bored with repetition. They are impatient with the practical. They make inspirational leaders, artists, and fashion designers. In industry, they often are responsible for starting up new companies, but when they are successful they may have to relinquish long-range management control to their more practical sensate counterparts.

According to Myers and Briggs, there are many more sensates than intuitives in the United States, and as a nation we value the practical more. The intuitive individual must put up with being evaluated by sensates, and must resist both the sensate's evaluation, and his own suspicion that the sensate may be "better." However, the intuitive is responsible for most of the art, poetry, spirituality, research, and imagination, without which this would certainly be a dull world. Jack Smith, a *Los Angeles Times* columnist, quotes a reader in his January 28, 1986 column as follows: "If we exiled all that is nifty, careless, wildly exaggerated, light-footed, vulnerable, or curiously spiced from our spiritual landscape, we would be in terrible shape." Really. I suspect he knows my wife.

Thinking and Feeling

Then there are the thinkers and feelers. The thinker is logical and organized, and comes to conclusions in an orderly, logical way. According to Myers and Briggs, thinkers have good analytical and critical ability, and think clearly, except when they believe that everyone should think the same way. Thinkers often do not understand or pay attention to the feelings of others. Much of the educational system is run by and geared to thinkers who see fact-gathering and clear-thinking as the ultimate objectives of education.

However, there are an equal number of feelers who are more comfortable coming to conclusions on the basis of feelings, and who are more sensitive to the emotional needs of others and of themselves. They develop strong beliefs and value systems that are non-negotiable. Their view of the world is built on the basis of what they consider right or good, and often they are willing to fight for these values. This generally upsets thinkers, who do not understand such emotional investment in non-logical beliefs.

There is considerable evidence that these differences may, at least in part, be culturally determined. For example, in one experiment, babies dressed in pink were cuddled more by women who didn't know them, than the same baby dressed in blue. One of my students who was a biochemistry major told us that one Christmas she was given a floppy doll by her uncle, and her brother received a chemistry set. Upon unwrapping the presents, they looked at each other, and exchanged gifts.

You can see, therefore, that if you are rooming with three other people, and if you are all different types, you might have trouble just deciding what to have for dinner!

Says the extrovert-intuitive, "O.K. everyone, lets all talk about all the possibilities."

Introvert-feeler: "I feel very strongly about a pepperoni pizza this evening."

Extrovert-sensate: "That sounds great. Good food, good friends, what more could anyone want?"

Introvert-thinker: "No good. Too much fat, not enough

nutrition. We need a more balanced diet. You guys just aren't thinking straight.''

And so it goes. If you can decide what to have for dinner in college, you may become a successful statesman, salesman, or negotiator . . .

The Mix Is Different In Each Of Us

In Appendix B I have included a chart with all the types. As you can see, there are sixteen possible combinations, but of course, people don't fall into neat packages, and we all are a mix of each of these characteristics. The mix is different in each of us, and it helps to know that there are different ways of doing things, and that one way is not better than another. Each has its own strengths. Not only is the other person's way of doing things all right, so is yours.

The important message is, that in this particular test there are no value judgments, there is no right or wrong, or better or worse type. The way you are is just the way you are, and is not up for evaluation by yourself or anyone else.

But there is a tradeoff here. On the one hand, it is really nice to find that there are other people who see the world the same way you do. With these people, you feel more comfortable, and you don't have to explain or defend yourself all the time.

However, people who see the world the same way tend to reinforce each other's beliefs that this is the way the world *should* be, and that everyone else is wrong. This is obviously not true. It is important to be able to get along with, respect, even grow to like, people who are not the same type and who see the world differently. It can lead to a more exciting life for you, and certainly a better rounded view of the world.

Furthermore, while you should certainly respect and believe in your own personality type, you should be open to the other values as well. An intuitive could benefit from cultivating an attention to detail and practicality, and a sensate could learn to do a little daydreaming. A feeler could learn to be more objective, and a thinker might learn to value the feelings of others. Growth involves learning to respect the way you are, and still remain open to change.

Some personality types are more comfortable in certain occupations and professions than in others. You might check with your school counselors about taking the full Myers-Briggs test so that you can compare your score with those in various occupations. It could help you with your career choices.

Your Unconscious

An important part of all of us is our unconscious. The unconscious is that part of our mind and body that functions without our being aware of it. For most of us our unconscious works smoothly and silently, without our even knowing it. Generally this is good; otherwise you would be like a centipede deciding which foot to move first. Conscious awareness is like a beam of light that illuminates only a small area of our "body-mind," and only a small part of us at any one time.

It requires effort to learn more about our unconscious, and when your psyche is functioning smoothly and all your legs are moving at the same time, it probably is not worth the trouble. But it is certainly worth exploring if you find yourself in trouble without knowing why. If, for example, you find yourself unduly distressed, depressed, or anxious, or doing things you know you shouldn't, it is advisable to explore your unconscious with the help of a guide from your counseling service.

Peggy, a young psychology student at Michigan State University, was engaged to a young man named Bill, but had just casually met another young man named Harold. One day she volunteered to be a subject at a class demonstration of automatic writing. Milton Erickson, a hypnotherapist, hypnotized her, and suggested she write something, anything, on a piece of paper. She wrote "Will I marry Harold?" But she folded it several times and put it in her bag. Then he gave her a post-hypnotic suggestion that when she awoke, she would write, "It's a beautiful day in June" (it was April). When she awoke, she did not mention hiding the first piece of paper in her bag, but took out a piece of paper and wrote "It's a beautiful day in June." This confused her, because she knew it was April.

It is, of course, only a coincidence that in June she broke off with Bill and become engaged to Harold. But when she then discovered the folded piece of paper in her bag, saying "Will I marry Harold?" she had no memory of ever writing it. She called Dr. Erickson, to ask him what it meant. He explained that a part of her knew in April that she wanted to marry Harold, but could not face breaking up with Bill at the time, so she folded the paper and hid it in her bag, until she was ready to face it.*

* Sidney Rosen, ed. *My Voice Will Go With You* (New York: W. W. Norton, 1982).*

The unconscious has a mind of its own. You can know things unconsciously that your conscious mind rejects. So the unconscious can be an interesting part of yourself to explore. It is somewhat like spelunking, where we explore deep caverns, and admire stalagmites, and are frightened by shadows; or like skin diving, where we see marvels that are hidden from those who see only the surface of the water.

Since we cannot look at the unconscious directly, we must look indirectly. Psychoanalysts use dreams, and word and thought association while the patient is lying in a semi-dark room. Meditation induces an altered state of consciousness that dips close to the unconscious. Some therapists use drugs or hypnosis to induce similar altered states of consciousness. For this purpose we can also use our own fantasy and imagery, as have many artists. Psychologist Dr. Joseph E. Shorr has written several books on the subject. One you might enjoy is called, *Go See the Movies in Your Head.* *

The next exercise in this book makes use of the psychological fact that people often identify deep bodies of water with their own unconscious. For example, when they describe the way they see an ocean, they often are creating a metaphor for the way they see themselves. One way to explore your unconscious, therefore, is in imagery, to explore a deep body of water, and to see what you find in it. If you find a fish, describe the fish; if you find a boot, describe the boot. The result will sometimes please you, and sometimes upset you; but it will almost always surprise you.

* 2nd. edition, (Los Angeles: Institute for Psycho-Imagination Therapy, 1983).

_____

EXERCISE 6. Exploring Your Unconscious

Purpose: To learn more about yourself.

Method: Make yourself comfortable. Relax all your muscles. In order to get into the right state of mind, imagine that you are going fishing on a beautiful day. You are walking along a dusty country road with a fishing pole. The meadows on each side are green, with many-colored flowers; the sky is blue; a few white clouds move along in the breeze which gently caresses your face.

You come to a lake, so deep that you cannot see the bottom. You throw your line and hook into the water and sit down to wait. As you move your line up and down, you suddenly feel something on it . . . What is it? You pull in your line . . . What have you caught? To understand its significance, Dr. Shorr has created some sentences about the object for you to complete. Imagine actually *being* the object, and, *as the object,* describe yourself by completing the following sentences:

> I feel . . .
> The adjective that best describes me is . . .
> I wish . . .
> I must . . .
> I secretly . . .
> I need . . .
> I will . . .
> Never refer to me as . . .

Comment: Until you actually do this exercise, you cannot imagine the incredible surprise your conscious mind may experience when faced with the products of your unconscious. For example, the completion of the statement "Never refer to me as . . ." may disclose some bad thought you have about yourself. That you were previously unaware of such a thought means that it was unconscious, and that this exercise brought it to consciousness. It may be associated with feelings you didn't know you had. If they disturb you unduly, it might be wise to talk to a counselor about them.

Dr. Shorr describes many such exercises, and each can be repeated many times, and each time will produce new images, new thoughts, and new feelings.

Valuing Your Individuality and Your Relationships

In Chapter I I mentioned John Bowlby's description of a child in the park with his mother. I made the point that he needed a good connection with her, in order to be able to go off and explore. We must have trust in our supportive relationships in order to be truly independent.

The best relationships are those in which each is free to express individuality. Somewhere between the extremes of over-socialization and alienation lies an area of true independence, where we can feel good about ourselves, and about our relationships also.

Too much dependency creates stress. If you feel too controlled by others, or are not sure of your own individuality, you may and should fight for symbols of freedom with passions that are not surprising, considering how basic these needs are. These symbols may range from clothes that express your own personality, to making speeches in the student council. But these symbols are, generally, only pathways. When you have achieved enough confidence in yourself, the pathways to it may stop being issues.

5 Self-Esteem

Jeff does not feel worthwhile. His parents are good, caring people. His father is a successful engineer who has parlayed several inventions into a small fortune. His mother is a busy psychotherapist. His brother performed brilliantly at Stanford, and is now in medical school. But Jeff feels he can't compete with his brother, or measure up to his parents' expectations; he lost that battle long ago. He feels there isn't any point in studying, because he isn't going to do well anyway. At nineteen, he is already a failure.

Jeff eagerly agrees with the requests and opinions of others; his own needs and opinions don't count much with him. He likes to make furniture (and is really very good at it), but doesn't see making furniture as having much value. *He* doesn't have much value in his own eyes. When his girlfriend, whom he really cared about, said she was thinking of moving to another city, he didn't fight for her. When people offered him drugs, he took them, and got messed up. He says, "It's all my fault. I did it to myself." He adds, "I'm pretty worthless."

The goals we set for ourselves are often intimately related to our self-image. What we expect of life depends on how we see ourselves. We may expect too little, or too much. We may be shackled by false ideas of our own limits, or we may set goals that exceed our abilities. Much of your future contentment or discontent will depend on your ability to set realistic goals for yourselves.

But do not tie your self-esteem to your goals. If you need to achieve merely to shore up your ego, you will be on a never-ending treadmill, running hard just to keep up.

I discovered this about myself in college when I took a test devised by Dr. Julian Rotter on a simple pinball machine (a mechanical device that antedated computer games). Before each game, we were required to estimate the number of points we thought we would make. We were penalized for any score below our estimate. No matter how well I understood this system, I found it almost impossible to lower my estimate for myself. I repeatedly set estimates above my actual, realistic performance, and ended up with a low, minus score. I was frustrated and humiliated.

And I learned a lot about myself and others. At first I thought I was the only one getting a low score. However, most of my classmates were also fighting the temptation to predict better performances than they could achieve.

So don't tie your self-esteem only to your scholastic or athletic achievements. If you need achievements to feel good about yourself, you will always be in trouble. Depending only on your scholastic skill and knowledge for your self-esteem is risky. It is nice to feel good about your ability to do well in school; in fact, it's great. But some people make that the major basis for their self-esteem. Don't. There are other more important reasons to feel good about yourself.

A test that measured self-esteem was given to people in many occupations. It was startling to find that janitors scored higher on this test than junior executives. Since janitors set lower goals for themselves, but achieved them, they had higher self-esteem than junior executives, who set higher goals that they had not achieved, at least so far. That doesn't mean that you should settle for being a janitor. At times, however, it may look tempting.

Self-Esteem is a Result of Learning and Decisions

There is probably no way to really know why Jeff feels so bad about himself, but in general self-esteem or it's lack comes from early learning experiences, and from decisions made as a result.

There are so many opportunities to feel good about yourself, or bad. There are many ways you can decide you are a good and worthwhile person, or not. Jeff's feeling of worthlessness could have begun very early in his life, even as a baby. Perhaps sometimes his mother wasn't there when he felt he needed her. Maybe she didn't smile at him when she was tired, or ignored him when he cried, and he began to believe there was something wrong with him. No one really knows why, in the same situation, some children decide there is something wrong with them, and others don't. Even if they can't remember this later, they make decisions about themselves at the time, deep in their non-verbal unconscious, that they still believe years later.

You too may believe decisions you made about yourself, decisions you made when you were so young you don't even remember the events. If, as a child, you believed you were stupid, you may still believe it, and prove it by doing things stupid people do.

Or you may believe that you are only as good as your latest achievements, so that you must spend your life getting good grades, being better than others, and generally proving yourself through your performance. Then you may develop "performance anxiety"; and if you fail to measure up to your internal standards, you feel inadequate.

Or your self-esteem may depend on what other people say about you. Do "they" say you are worthwhile? Good looking? Likable? Clever? You may constantly try to please others, a futile occupation.

All these episodes and decisions may help explain why you feel the way you do about yourself now; and now, looking back, you have the opportunity to re-evaluate your decisions. If you can recognize yourself in the above description, even a little, this chapter is important to you.

On the other hand, you may be one of the "invulnerables." The "invulnerables" were a group of children in New York who, growing up in the worst possible economic and social circumstances, with parents who did all the worst things and with no opportunity to learn good behavior, still grew up feeling good about themselves. Recently there has been another study of children who grew up in Nazi concentration camps. Many turned into good, upstanding, achieving, motivated adults, with good jobs and marriages. Although torn from their families at an early age, and growing up with fear, deprivation, and degradation, they somehow *decided* they were O.K., and have since behaved accordingly. How did they do this? We don't really know. Somehow the "invulnerables" *know* they are good people. Their sense of self-esteem is non-negotiable. It does not depend on other people or on external circumstances.

How High is Your Self-Esteem?

Your own self-esteem may indeed be high; it may even be *very* high. However, there aren't that many invulnerables. By the time we leave childhood, almost all of us can use some help with our self-esteem.

In this and the next two chapters I will present some exercises that help improve self-esteem. They will help you

1. increase your sense of being a good person "no matter what,"

2. be more assertive, and

3. reduce an unrealistic sense of guilt and inadequacy.

One way to improve self-esteem is to internalize a good self-image that you can reactivate in times of stress and anxiety. The following exercise, will help you increase your sense of being a good person "no matter what."

EXERCISE 7. Anchoring Good Feelings

Purpose: To internalize and anchor good feelings about yourself.

Method: When you are actually experiencing good, warm, self-approving feelings, take a few minutes to "anchor" them. These feelings may occur when you have done something especially well and you are pleased with yourself, when you are in love, when you are lying on the beach, feeling good about the world, or when someone important to you is saying nice things about you. You can also do this in a fantasy, as you imagine or remember these things, and experience these good feelings. Whatever the occasion, take the good feelings in, experience them fully. Also experience fully whatever sensations you may have: the sight of people's expressions, the sound of their voices, the sensation of your own facial expression, sensations in your skin and body.

While you are doing this, squeeze your upper left arm with your right hand, firmly. That's all. While you are experiencing your good feelings, squeeze your upper left arm firmly with your right hand. Then, any time you need to recall these feelings, touch your left arm again with your right hand. Like magic, the associations will be made, the connection will be reestablished, and the good feelings about yourself will flood through you.

Comment: Like most magic, once this is explained, it stops being magic. It turns out that the body as well as the brain has a memory which can be recalled by the appropriate action. Bandler and Grinder have written extensively about this phenomenon *(Frogs into Princes).** Athletes know this; when they have a perfect performance, they let their body remember what they did. When you are taking a test and can't remember the answer, you may recall the material easier if you assume the posture you had when you were reading it. The body's sensations are an important part of your memories.

Assertiveness

In order to increase your sense of self-esteem, not only must you feel like a good person, you must act like one. You must express in your actions that you are worthwhile, not just so others will think you are, but so *you* will think you are. Beliefs are both the cause of and the result of behaviors. When you see yourself being assertive, you will find yourself feeling good about yourself. If, on the other hand, you act and talk like a rug, people will walk on you, and you will feel like a rug.

* (Moab, Utah: Real People Press, 1979).

What is Assertiveness?

Imagine two students who have been assigned a room in a dormitory. One comes in, picks the bed by the window, and throws his/her bag on it. Shortly after, the other student comes in, looks the room over, and cheerfully says, "I really like a window by my bed. How would you feel about trading beds?" The first student, startled and taken aback, says, "Sure, I wouldn't mind."

Which student are you?

Let us start by defining assertiveness, so that we are sure we are talking about the same thing.

Assertiveness is 1) the ability to say what you think, what you feel, what you want for yourself, 2) without aggressiveness 3) and without anxiety, 4) with respect for the other person, 5) in such a way that you have a good chance of getting what you want, 6) when it is appropriate.

What do these words mean? More important, what do they mean to you?

1. *The ability to say what you want for yourself, and what you think and feel.* Would that be a good thing? Being able to say these things depends on your feelings that what you have in your heart and mind is important enough to say out loud, and that *you* are important enough to say it.

2. *Without aggressiveness.* Aggressiveness is obnoxious. It implies that your needs are more important than that of others, or if you aren't aggressive, no one will pay attention to you. It may get you what you want, but it is very bad for your relationships.

3. *Without anxiety.* Anxiety is the main reason we are not more assertive. We want others to like us and to think well of us. We are afraid they won't. We are afraid of consequences, consequences that are usually unrealistic but frightening anyway. We are afraid of being punished in some way.

4. *With respect for the other person.* Respect is communicated to the other person by listening carefully to the other's needs and feelings, and acknowledging and affirming them, without implying that they are more or less important than yours.

5. *In such a way that there is a good chance of getting what you want.* This means speaking firmly and pleasantly, but not demanding. Being assertive will usually get you what you want; but you don't act assertively *in order* to get what you want. That's aggressive, not assertive. You can live without filling all your needs all the time.

6. Finally, *when it is appropriate* implies *choice* on your part. You never *need* to be assertive; you always have to decide that it is appropriate. When an eighty-year old lady with a heavy bundle pushes into line ahead of you, you can decide to let her; you don't have to assert yourself. And it's not smart to practice being assertive with insecure people in positions of power. For example, some insecure teachers are threatened by assertive students. Most people with power, however, are not insecure and will welcome assertiveness on your part.

In our society, the feelings and concerns of children are often not valued or even given credence. You may have been brought up in the "martyr mode," to believe that you should put the needs of others far ahead of your own. If you are a woman you may have been brought up to believe that you should just be a good listener and a caring helper. Some social attitudes die hard, and women especially often find it hard to be pleasantly assertive. But you must be able to speak your thoughts and feelings about your needs in order to function effectively. If you don't say what you want for yourself, the chances of getting it are small.

My wife and I once were the "parents" of Mark, an exchange student from Tasmania (an Australian island). One evening he stayed late at school to attend a concert. At about ten o'clock he phoned us to come and get him because everyone had gone home. "Why," we asked, "didn't you get a ride with someone? Lots of students live near us." "Well," he answered, "I stood by the door and waited, but no one asked me." Tasmanians apparently function differently. You don't get too many rides in this country by standing at the door, waiting to be asked.

Mark was a quick study, however. Two months later he was running for class president. But he wrote us a letter after he returned home, saying it was difficult for him to readjust to the Tasmanian way of doing things; his old friends now found him "Americanized."

Learning to be Assertive

For most of us, however, assertiveness is not that easy, if you are not used to it. In order to become assertive you are going to have to practice. It is best if you practice with another person who will role-play different people saying different things. It is even better if you have a whole group of people, each giving you different responses. It is also very important that you start with the gentlest person giving you the best response possible, and then *gradually* confront more difficult people giving you more and more unpleasant responses, until you are finally able to be assertive with anyone about anything. Just don't start off trying to be assertive with the most difficult person giving you the worst possible response.

Begin by thinking of a circumstance in which you have not been saying what you want for yourself. Perhaps your new roommate (the one with the bed by the window) now leaves wet towels on your bed and turns up the stereo while you are trying to study. Most people are not either assertive or non-assertive; instead, there are circumstances or people who make it especially difficult for us to say what we want for ourselves. Think about the circumstance and the person; what exactly is it that you would like to say? What makes it hard to say? What is the worst response that anyone could give you?

Almost always, it is what people *might possibly* say to or about you that is the stumbling block. What you tell yourself people are going to say is what keeps you from being assertive. As you think about those painful remarks, you probably are developing some uncomfortable feelings.

Suds (Subjective Units of Discomfort)

Assertiveness trainers call these uncomfortable feelings SUDS, which is an acronym for Subjective Units of Discomfort. SUDS come when you fear awful consequences. SUDS is shorthand for breaking out in a cold sweat, having your muscles cramp down in your head, your neck, or your back; feeling your heart race; feeling a knot in your stomach; or just wishing the earth would open up and swallow you. SUDS mean you have just said goodbye to your chances of ever being happy again. SUDS are awful feelings. It is no wonder that you avoid them by not speaking up and saying what you want for yourself.

Later, when your SUDS are low again, you kick your-self. "I could have said this. I should have said that!" No, sorry, you couldn't. Your SUDS were too high.

Assertiveness training increases assertiveness by sys-tematically reducing SUDS. In order to do this, you first need to actually measure your SUDS on the following rough scale.

SUDS SCALE

0–10: You are alert and mildly excited. Your mind is clear, you think rapidly and remember well. (E.g., you are talking with a good friend.)

20: You feel tense but are functioning well. (Two at-tractive people of the opposite sex are walking toward you.)

30: You are distinctly uncomfortable. The situation is becoming difficult and you would rather be somewhere else. (They stop, smile, and start to chat with your friend who fails to introduce you.)

40: Your mind is turning off; you can't think, you can't remember, and you feel you're making a fool of yourself. (You start to introduce yourself, but for some reason be-come tongue-tied, and can't remember your own name.)

50: You look for ways to reduce the discomfort. You start defending, explaining, justifying, attacking, and blaming others for the way you feel. (Anyway, these peo-ple are really stupid; you wouldn't be caught dead talking with them.)

60: You withdraw, escape, hide. You become rigid and shell-like; your responses become stereotyped. (You are totally unconcerned, and as soon as they leave you will drown yourself in a vat of suds.)

70: Personality disintegration begins. You can no longer handle the world or your own affairs. (You begin to hit your head against a tree and throw rocks through windows.)

80: Psychotic behavior, an escape from reality, is the only course available. (They take you away to the hospital, babbling and hysterical, a pitiable object. However with sympathetic counseling and a good night's sleep you may return to normal.)

90: Psychotic changes are permanent; brain damage is irreversible. (They lock you up and throw away the key.)

100: Total humiliation and heartbreak. (The worst possible stage known to college students.)

SUDS levels of 30 and 40 are the usual levels at which most college students meet faculty (when they become tongue-tied and stupid), and take exams (when they can't remember something they know perfectly as soon as they leave the classroom.)

Don't confuse what we are going to do in these first few exercises with real life. These are *practice* exercises, to practice with friends. They will help you with real situations, but they are not themselves the real situations. In order to lower your SUDS, we will do some things in these exercises that might not be appropriate in a classroom.

For example, for these exercises, *we won't evaluate your thoughts and wants.* They can be as irrational and unreasonable as you wish. We will pretend that you are entitled to want and say anything; your wants and beliefs are non-negotiable! If you wish, you can ask for a Citroen Maserati, or As without working, or a million dollars.

We're not talking reality here. Of course, you may not *get* whatever it is you want, but in these exercises you are certainly entitled to *ask*.

During these exercises, you also know that your partner is really on your side and that you are only role-playing.

EXERCISE 8. Asking and Getting

Purpose: To increase assertive behavior.

Method: Start by saying something simple to your partner that you have wanted to say to someone, and have not. Make it into a short statement. Say it out loud. (E.g., "I would like you to keep your wet towels off my bed.")

Notice how uncomfortable you feel, and what your voice sounds like.

Ask your partner to say something you would *like* to hear. Not what she really thinks or is likely to say, but what *you want* her to say. After all, this is only role-playing, you are in charge, and you can have her say *anything you want.* What would that be? "Of course! I didn't realize! I'm glad you told me. I'll certainly keep my wet towels off your bed.)"

Comment: As you hear what you would like to hear, what happens to your SUDS? Do they come down?

It'll never happen? Maybe, maybe not. Remember, this is only role-playing; it's not supposed to be totally realistic. It is supposed to make you feel less uncomfortable about saying what you want. Does hearing what you would like to hear make you feel *more* uncomfortable? It does, sometimes. Try the same scenario again several more times. Say what you want, and have your friend say *what you would like to hear.* Your discomfort should decrease, to be replaced by a rather pleasant and enjoyable feeling.

If it didn't happen, it might be because you didn't ask for enough. Maybe you wanted something else instead. Maybe you wanted a better and fuller apology. Go ahead—ask. Hearing what you would like to hear, and getting what you want, even as role-playing, can be a wonderful experience!

EXERCISE 9. Negative Responses

Purpose: To deal with negative responses.

Method: Most people would like to stop here, because it feels so good. In real life, if you ask assertively, there is a good chance the other person will actually say what you want to hear. But in order to be able to ask assertively, with low SUDS, you have to be able to deal with less than perfect responses. So let's practice hearing and responding to the things that may or may not be said, but for which you must be prepared. What are some other responses people might possibly make?

Tell your partner some of the responses you wouldn't like. Start with responses that you might be able to handle well. Don't suggest the worst right away. Make the first few responses very mild.

Then check out your SUDS. If someone said or thought these things, how uncomfortable would you be? What happens to your SUDS? Give your SUDS a number. For example, if you asked your friend not to put wet towels on your bed your friend might say, "I'm sorry, but your bed is closer to the sink." (Remember, this is only your friend.) So you check out your SUDS, and they're up to 70 (because you can't think, and also you feel like throwing your friend out the window.)

O.K., what do you do now? Now you play a "broken record."

THE BROKEN RECORD

What is a "broken record?" In its simplest form, the broken record means 1) to affirm the other person, and then 2) repeat what you said.

1. *Affirm the other person.* You remember we talked about affirming the other person in chapter III. Repeat enough of what you heard to make sure that the other person knows you heard. You don't have to believe it; you're just letting them know you're listening. Say it in a respectful manner, and try to make the other person know that you are not criticizing or blaming them. "Play back" what you heard.

"My bed *is* closer to the sink . . ."

2. Then finish the sentence by repeating your request: ". . . but I really would like you not to put wet towels on my bed."

Simple to read, but you may have trouble saying it, or even remembering it. When we are uncomfortable, *our minds turn off.* It is a common experience. If this is happening to you, don't be alarmed or embarrassed—just repeat the same interchange with your friend, using the same words, three or four times, until you have it down pat, your SUDS are down, and you are no longer so uncomfortable.

However, after you are comfortable with this, you are still not through. You still have to deal with worse statements. Gradually give your partner worse and worse ammunition to shoot at you. Each time, check your SUDS level, then repeat the gist of that statement, and then, *without responding to it,* go back and say what it is you want. E.g., to "You know, you're really strange!" answer, "I know I'm strange, and I'd still like you not to put wet towels on my bed." "You're not a very nice person." "I'm probably not a nice person, and I'd still like you not to put wet towels on my bed." "You're short and ugly." "I am short and ugly, and I'd like you not to put wet towels on my bed." Etc. etc.

Comment: You will notice three very interesting things happening in this exercise. In the first place, you will find yourself bringing up a lot of negative things about yourself that you have not previously verbalized, junk that you have been carrying around without even knowing it. Just saying these things out loud lets the wind carry them away so that they are no longer burdens.

The second interesting thing is that as your SUDS diminish, your voice becomes firmer, your mood becomes more cheerful, and your mind becomes inventive. You think of things to say that may surprise and delight you. You become spontaneous, and allow new thoughts and responses to come out into the open. (You might, for example, decide to go into the bathroom, return with a sopping wet towel, and ask, "Your bed or mine?") Enjoy yourself. But don't forget to end up with your statement of *what you want.*

The third interesting thing that happens is that you stop being afraid to hear the terrible things the other person says. When you listen to something, over and over, without having to do something about what you heard, without defending yourself or justifying what you want, the words you hear lose their power to make you anxious. You even may get a little bored with them, and wonder, "Why did that ever bother me?" You even begin to enjoy being able to hear the worst things possible without flinching, and with a fast and funny comeback. It is only fear that keeps you from saying what you want for yourself. Get these fears out in the open. You may like the feeling of being in charge of yourself, and not being destroyed by these terrible responses, imaginary or real. You may have a new feeling of freedom.

Remember, this is only role-playing. It may be different in the real world, but we will get to that later. For now, just keep repeating these interchanges; and when you become comfortable, have your friend make statements that make you more and more uncomfortable, letting you deal with them, one at a time.

Questions, or, "That's Not the Point"

You may not believe this, but you don't have to answer any questions from anyone, if they make you feel defensive. Questions may just be a way of asking you for information. On the other hand, questions can also be used as a way of saying, "Tell me why you did what you did, so I can tell you how stupid you are!"

You may have been trained as a child to answer that kind of interrogation by explaining and justifying yourself, to yourself and others. *You just don't have to.* Remember, we said that for the purposes of these exercises, what you want is non-negotiable, and you don't have to defend or justify yourself. You certainly don't have to give away the power to decide your fate to others. You don't have to let others decide if what you want is reasonable. You don't have to explain why you want something, only to have the other person say, "That's not a good enough reason."

So, if a question diverts you from being assertive by asking you to justify your motives, change your response to: *"That's not the point . . ."* and *". . . and I would like* etc. etc." Tattoo that response on your hand and in your heart. "That's not the point . . ."

Threats, or, "What You Do Is Up To You"

Some people use threats, because threats work. All behaviors have consequences, but threats go beyond the normal consequences of behavior; they link simple requests or demands with awful consequences. They create concern, so people may give in rather than take the chance that the threat will be delivered. When threats work, they establish a very unpleasant kind of relationship, with arrogant control on one side, and resentful compliance on the other. Be aware of threats; identify them immediately for what they are, an unacceptable attempt to control your behavior.

Threats may take various forms, from "If you're going to make a fuss about a simple thing like a towel, I'll really soak your bed," to "If you say that once more I'll throw you out the window." If the consequence exceeds the circumstance, by far, it is a threat. Once you have identified the demand as a threat, no matter how much you fear the consequences, you must never, ever, give in. It only reinforces that kind of behavior; you will then have to face it again and again.

Remind yourself that there is only a very small chance that what is threatened will actually happen. Then take the wind out of their sail with a very simple answer. Always respond to a threat with a broken record, like "I can see how important this is to you," and then end with "and *you have to do what is right for you,*" or, *"What you do is up to you."*

On the other hand, there are three situations where I would advise you not to call people's bluff. Don't call the "bluff" of a teacher who is threatening to fail you if you don't show up in class. Don't stand up to a "crazy," like people who threaten you on the road; roll up your window and drive away. And if someone threatens to kill themselves, don't ignore the threat, and don't try to handle it yourself; call a Suicide Prevention Center.

Insults and "Put-Downs"

For negative expressions like insults, you have two good choices. First, don't argue or defend yourself; and don't start trading insults. Agree, but then carry the agreement even further than the other person intended. "You're a slime-bag." "I'm the worst slime-bag in the world. My mother threw me into the trash and put the lid on so I wouldn't stink up the neighborhood. And I'd like you to not put your wet towels on my bed." Very effective.

Or, you can respond, not to the content of the words, but to the emotion, or to the *process* of the interchange. "You're a slimebag." "I can see I have upset you and you're angry . . ." And always end up with ". . . but I would like etc., etc."

Hearing "No"

Finally, you have to accept that sometimes you are not going to get what you want. Asking for what you want assertively makes it likely that you *will* get what you ask for, most of the time. The rest of the time you have to be able to hear "No," without coming apart at the seams. You have to deal with that irrational feeling that you *should* get what you want simply because you ask for it.

What do you do if, after saying what you want, you don't get it?

Run the "broken record" once; *just once.* Acknowledge what the other person said, and say once again what you want. If it doesn't work, accept that you are not going to get what you want from that person. If it doesn't work, don't keep trying. Sometimes you can't get what you want from some people, no matter how justified you are.

People are wonderfully creative when they are not paralyzed by anxiety. Hearing "No" may be unpleasant, but it is rarely the end of the world. Be prepared with alternatives. Just think, "O.K. That avenue is blocked; what do I do now?" You'll think of something if your SUDS are low.

If you practice this, by the end of half an hour of hard work you should be able to respond to *anything* your friends can throw at you with low SUDS. If it seems unreasonable to you that you can change so much in half an hour—well, try it before you decide.

The Real World

But this has all been with your friends. What happens in the real world?

The experience generalizes. You will find it easier to speak up for yourself. But the rules out there are a little different.

1. Practice makes perfect. At the start, pick easy situations where you are pretty sure nothing terrible will happen, and you'll get what you want easily. Give yourself some good experiences before you start being assertive with your teacher. Don't practice on policemen, judges, and deans. Leave them for later.

2. *Always remember to carefully acknowledge and validate the communication and feelings of the person with whom you are talking.* This is absolutely essential for good relationships. Don't get so hooked into answering them that you run over their feelings. Play back what they said very carefully; they, too, have a right to what they want and think.

3. In "real life," *never play the broken record more than twice!* It becomes aggressive. You may indeed get what you want, but at the expense of good relationships. That's not the name of this game. Be able to hear and respect "No!"

Now we get to the nitty-gritty. Now we get to what happens when you actually want to say something in a difficult situation.

Well, it turns out to be easy. All this practice has cleared out the fantasies about the worst that could happen and the anxieties about how that might make you feel. You've already taken care of all that. Now you should be able to say what you want for yourself without having your SUDS go through the roof. And you'll also have the tools to deal with whatever the other person says. All you have to do is to play the broken record *once,* and then, when your SUDS are down, you can *think!* You will be in charge of your alternatives.

Remember, you mustn't just practice this exercise with friends you trust. After you are comfortable with friends, take it into the real world. Practice with the other people in your life. It takes a lot of practice for you to become naturally and spontaneously assertive. But it will be worth it; the payoff will be increased self-esteem and feelings of self-worth.

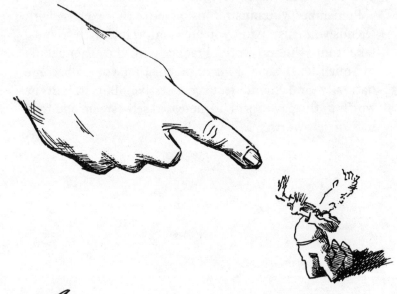

6 Criticism

L et's listen in on Sociology 101.

Instructor: "Mr. Brown, you had some interesting ideas in your paper. However, your spelling is so atrocious I can't pass it. Have you considered a word processor with a spelling checker?"

Mr. Brown cringes, and smiles weakly.

"Miss Gray, your paper was so confusing I couldn't understand what it was you were trying to say. Please rewrite it with an outline of your ideas. Do you know how to make an outline?"

Miss Gray gets a little red on the back of her neck, but nods.

"Mr. Green, your paper was better than last week. I think you're beginning to understand what this class is about, but you still have a long way to go."

Mr. Green freezes while he thinks that one over. It sounded like a compliment, but he's not sure.

No one likes to be criticized, but the higher you go in education the more it will happen. Most teaching is by feedback; you say or do something, and the teacher comments or corrects. If there is nothing for the teacher to add, there is nothing for you to learn.

Do you find criticism unsettling? I think everyone does. Often we get so defensive that we can't take a valid criticism and use it. We can be wiped out by a casual comment about the structure of a sentence, or the way we use commas. When something we have done is being criticized, we feel *we* are being criticized.

Fortunately, there is a way to accept and use criticism, without being defensive or feeling humiliated.

In order to do this, you must first take a good look at what criticism means to you. Criticism often carries more than one message. Usually there are three messages. 1. What you did leaves room for improvement. 2. In addition, you are stupid, inadequate, and probably hopeless, and everyone is laughing at you. 3. Besides, good people always get things right the first time, so probably you are a "bad person."

The first message, that you left room for improvement, isn't so bad by itself. After all, that's why you came to college, isn't it? If you already know everything you need to know, what are you doing here?

No, it's the second two messages that give the trouble. We tend to identify ourselves with what we do; there is a part of *us* that is being evaluated. Especially when we are doing something creative, like writing an essay, we put ourselves into what we have done. When our creation is praised, *we* feel praised. When it is criticized, *we* feel criticized. People may say, "Don't take it personally." Hah! We *always* take it personally.

Furthermore, there is always a voice inside of us, an inner critic, that echoes these messages, and adds, "I *told* you so! I told you, you are *bad.*" We all have this inner critic who quickly agrees with anything bad about us. In fact, *nothing anyone says about us hurts unless our inner critic agrees.* Oh, we may be upset and outraged by unfair criticism, but the real hurt and humiliation only occurs when our inner critic agrees: "You know, they're right! You're a terrible person."

Where does this last message come from? Let me tell you a story that is a metaphor for what happens to children as they grow up. It may explain why criticism is so difficult for you now.

The Native's God: A Metaphor

Imagine an island in the South Pacific inhabited by natives who have had no contact with "civilization." They have their own belief system they never question. For example they "know" their god is all-powerful, and they "know" he has their best interests at heart.

One day there is a tsunami, a storm that drives a wave forty feet high over their island. A native, clinging to the top of a tall, wind-tossed palm tree, watches his village destroyed, his pigs washed out to sea, and his family drown. He can see how powerful his god is. Into his mind comes the question, "If our god is so powerful, why does this happen?" The idea that this all-powerful god is *not* good, or may even be indifferent, is much too frightening to even contemplate. Instead, he must believe that he, the native, did something wrong. Therefore, as soon as the storm is over, he thinks of *something* he did to offend his god, builds a fire and sacrifices some valuable object to him (preferably living). Then he promises to behave better in the future. This makes him feel much better.

Powerful Parents

This is a metaphor for what really happens to small children. When we are little, we still believe our parents are all-powerful, and have our best interests at heart. Then one day there is a catastrophe. Perhaps our "god" is irritable and spanks us. A child must believe he did something wrong. He looks back and decides that whatever he was doing just before the spanking, was wrong. He cries, promises to do better, and feels better. He has developed the "awareness" of not being "good." He has developed a conscience and sense of guilt.

I remember being infuriated once in a restaurant as I saw a small child, barely able to stand, get down from her chair, and get slapped and pulled back; reach for some food from her mother's plate and get slapped; start to cry and get slapped, and then cling to her mother's neck and get slapped. The memory of that helpless, bewildered infant still enrages me.

That is not an extreme case, and it is easy for infants to get the idea that they are "bad." Given the unrealistic standards of behavior that parents expect (that the children later expect of themselves), and the traumas and punishments that are visited upon them when they fail, "being bad" makes sense to them.

"You Bad Child!"

Unchanged wet diapers and unappeased hunger, parental angers, slaps, spankings, and charges of "bad child!" all make it easy for children to believe in their own evil nature.

Thinking they are bad is less frightening than feeling helpless in a world inhabited by irresponsible powerful giants with unattainable ideals of behavior, who allow or even cause catastrophes. They must believe that the catastrophes were a punishment for being bad. This allows them to think that they are exercising some control and by making amends, they can possibly alter the malignant course of events.

"I Never Praised Them When They Were Good."

Parents who say nothing as long as things are going well and who teach good behavior only by pointing out the bad, confirm this evaluation. In a behavioral therapy clinic for "problem children" I was doubtful at first about giving the children "tokens" (plastic coins) for any behavior judged good by the psychologist. I asked one of the mothers, "What do you think of this kind of therapy?" She answered, "It's made me realize that I never never said anything good to them when they were good. I just yelled at them when they were doing something wrong. Maybe that's why they turned into 'problem children.'" And then she added, "And you know, I can't remember my mother ever praising anything I ever did. Maybe that's why I never praised my children. I just didn't know you were supposed to."

Guilt

Parents also use guilt because it works; it gives them control. Children "behave" in order to remove the shame of their parents' disapproval. In due course they will "behave" in order to avoid their own (their internalized parents') disapproval. When "behaving" conflicts with their own true nature and needs, the groundwork is set for emotional difficulties that have made mental health one of the preeminent problems of our generation. It sometimes takes years of therapy before people can see themselves as good people, and not as rotten little kids.

Many of us grow up, then, often willing to believe we are "bad" in order to make sense out of an otherwise frighteningly hostile or indifferent world. We are quick to put ourselves down, and sometimes even do self-destructive things we would never think of doing if we felt better about ourselves. We also grow up needing to avoid the awful pain that this terrible illusion of badness causes. We do this by defending, explaining, and justifying; by denying, repressing, and presenting a "good image."

Rarely do we actually face, confront, and dispel this illusion.

While the instructor in Soc. 101 is thinking, "What a wonderful thing I am doing, by pointing out my students' shortcomings to them," the students are thinking, "Now everyone knows how bad I am."

The instructor is thinking, "I am helping the students by pointing out where they need to improve, and even giving them some helpful suggestions, and encouragement. I wonder why they don't like me more?"

He doesn't even suspect that Mr. Brown heard, "You're atrocious! You're atrocious!" Miss Gray is thinking, "Outline—outline—how do you make an outline? Everyone heard him say I'm too stupid to belong in college." And Mr. Green hears, "Long way to go . . . long way to go . . . He doesn't think I'll make it."

Later, Brown asks Gray, "How about lunch?" Gray thinks, "He heard the instructor say I'm stupid, and he just wants to make me feel better. No, thanks," and counters, "I'd like to, but I have to go to the library." Brown asks, "Maybe tomorrow?" thinking, "She doesn't want to be seen with me. I guess she agrees I'm atrocious."

. And so it goes.

The Lash of Our Own Critics

I said earlier that nothing anyone says about us hurts unless our inner critic agrees. Nobody's scorn, criticism, or anger would matter so much if our own internal critics did not rush to agree. In addition, nothing that can happen to us, in the world or in college, is as *painful* as our own internal critics telling us how bad we are. No matter what the consequences of our action, or what anyone says to us, it is magnified manyfold by the emotions of guilt, shame, humiliation, inadequacy, and embarrassment that our own critics evoke in us. Anxiety is provoked, not so much by the fear of terrible consequences, as by the fear of the lash of our own critics that accompany those consequences. Consequences may be bad, but our critics make them worse.

In Chapter V you worked on the "broken record," in which you said what you wanted for yourself, listened carefully to another person's response, checked out your SUDS level, and then repeated your original statement. You also tried some appropriate responses to questions, threats, insults, and hearing "No."

Now, I want you to start reducing your SUDS level to criticism.

EXERCISE 10. Reducing Fear of Criticism

Purpose: To reduce the discomfort caused by criticism, so as to handle and use it better.

Method: Find at least two other people to help you work on criticism. At least one of these people should be a kind, gentle friend. The word "work" is used advisedly, because this can be a difficult exercise. It is normal to freeze into immobility and forgetfulness when you experience criticism. Therefore, someone has to role-play criticising you, and someone has to help you remember what to do.

As I said, our critics evoke in us feelings of guilt, shame, embarrassment, humiliation and inadequacy. Our fear of experiencing these feelings is felt as anxiety. However, for our purposes, you need not identify the exact feeling criticism causes in you. Rather, I want you just to identify your SUDS level. You will remember, I am sure, how your SUDS feel to you. Your body posture changes, your muscles tense, your hands get clammy, your breathing changes, your heart pounds, your stomach feels sick. Just put any or all of these physical responses together, call them SUDS, and give them a numerical value on the SUDS scale.

Start by telling your partners of a recent situation in which you were criticized, and how it made you feel. Start with something mild. Perhaps someone said something derogatory about your social skills, something like "You blew it, kid. We can't take you anywhere!"

Say what your SUDS level was at the time, what they are now as you recall the incident, and what they rise to as your *critical* partner repeats the derogatory statement.

Notice also the strong temptation to hit back verbally, to leave, to joke, or to "dexify" (defend, explain, and justify.) Don't. Inhibit these impulses. Just sit there with your SUDS, whatever they are.

Before you respond, take a second to relax your body, and to reassure yourself that you are still O.K. Anchor a good feeling by squeezing your left arm with your right hand, as in exercise 7. You have to have already done this exercise in order to be able to use it now. If you haven't already done that exercise, do it now before proceeding.

Then play the broken record as follows: "I blew it, and you can't take me anywhere." Then add, *"And* I am still a good person." If you have any trouble saying this, your *supporting* partner can prompt you, and reassure you.

Repeat this broken record, over and over and over, until you can reply with a very low SUDS level. Then go to more and more obnoxious critical statements, and play the broken record each time, until nothing that your *critical* partner can say will raise your SUDS!

Comment: In order to be able to handle criticism and to use it well, it is necessary to be able to hear it without flinching. To do this, you have to gag your internal critic who keeps saying, "You see, I told you so!" The truth is, *you are a good person, and sometimes you do stupid things,* and make mistakes, and display ignorance and lack of experience, and a hundred other human behaviors. Doing these things does *not* make you a bad person. They are all only *learning experiences.* Wisdom comes from experience, and experience means doing stupid things and making mistakes and learning from them. It is even all right to disbelieve your first experience and check it out again. Just don't make the same mistake three times; try new ways when the old ones don't work.

You will know you really believe you are O.K. when your instructor says to you "You really did a terrible job" and you can respond, "Yeah, I know," and your SUDS don't go up. You will have dissociated criticism from your own feeling of worth. You won't even have to squeeze your arm and tell yourself, "and I am a good person."

Learn from Experience

You also have to stop defending yourself by insisting you are "right." Whether you are right or not has nothing whatever to do with whether or not you are a good person. Contrary to general opinion, there is no such thing in life as doing things "right" or "perfectly." Life is a continuous, ongoing process of learning. You learn from your experience. One of the most valuable experiences you can have is to be critiqued by someone knowledgeable. In this process, you must be open to the feedback. Defensiveness, anger, resentment, hurt, embarrassment, humiliation— all of these get in your way. When you defend, justify, and explain, you are blocking your own growth.

Constructive vs. Destructive Criticism

Up until now, we have been talking mainly about constructive criticism. Of course, not all criticism is constructive, justified or valid. Sometimes criticism is used as a way of expressing hostility.

The difference between constructive criticism and destructive criticism is that constructive criticism is concerned with helping you do things better. Destructive criticism is telling you that your internal critics are right, *you're not a good person.* If a criticism is bothering you, listen very carefully; who is telling you you're not O.K.? You, or the other person? If it's you, you can reassure yourself, and deal with your own internal critic. But if it really is the other person who is telling you you're not O.K., you have to be able to reassure yourself, and then deal with the other person.

Unfortunately, there are some aggressive, hostile people out there who are not your friends. They may use criticism as a weapon to try to make you do what they want, or even just to make you feel bad. To deal with them successfully, you must have successfully graduated from the previous criticism exercise so that your SUDS are not excessive, and you can think. Remember, when your SUDS are high, your mind turns off. Then, you must be able to identify the individual as hostile.

Many well-meaning people make critical remarks; you don't have to respond to them the same way you do to people who are using criticism to hurt or manipulate you. Sometimes people who are otherwise nice will dump on you. Your roommate may have had a bad experience last night, and your teacher may have been fighting with his wife. These are not hostile people; don't use the tools I am about to describe on them.

EXERCISE 11. Coping with Hostile, Critical People

Purpose: To deal with *hostile* critical remarks.
Method:
1. Don't "Dexify."*
I mentioned this before. A hostile person immediately "has you" if you try to *defend, explain,* or *justify* your actions or position. You are asking a hostile person to accept your worth. Give up on that before you even start.
2. Play the broken record.
I said earlier to use the broken record (validate and then say what you want) only once or twice, and then stop. Continuing it further is aggressive; it may get you what you want, but it is bad for relationships. Well, this is an exception. It is great for dealing with aggressive or hostile

*My thanks to Jerry Greenwald, Ph.D., who coined this term.

people. Validate what they are saying, don't respond to it, and then just say what you want. Do it over and over. Validate the hell out of them, but don't respond, and always repeat what you want. "Would you let Shirley know I'm here, please?" "Shirley wouldn't want to talk to a wimp like you." "Shirley probably wouldn't want to talk to a wimp like me, but I would like you to tell her I'm here, please." "Wimps like you bug me; get lost." "I understand you don't like wimps, and I'd like you to tell Shirley I'm here, now, please." "You're an idiot and you don't understand English." "I'm probably an idiot and my understanding of English is deficient, and I'd like you to call Shirley now, please." It is an impregnable position, and your attacker will soon get tired of the game.

3. Do a "content-process shift."

Learning to do a content-process shift is easier than it sounds. *Content* refers to the literal meaning of the words that are said. If someone shrieks "You're an idiot!", the content is that you're an idiot, I.Q. 40. *Process* refers to the interpersonal or psychological process that is going on. For example, he's excited, upset, angry, blaming, deprecating, shrieking, and probably a dozen other things. Take your pick. Instead of validating what the other person says, you comment on the process of the interchange. For example, you obviously are not going to get anywhere by defending your I.Q. Instead you say, "I can see you're upset with me."

Addressing *process* helps you confront the basic interpersonal relationship; you change the focus to that of two people with something to work out.

A content-process shift is a positive act. It reduces tension, facilitates communication, and improves relationships. The next technique, however, is hostile, aggressive, and terrible for relationships. Try it once or twice, and then put it away. Just knowing that you have this weapon may give you enough confidence so that you can keep it in your back pocket—and never need to take it out.

4. If all else fails, FOG

Fogging means that with rapt attention, you just agree with everything that is said, and promise nothing. "Oh, yes; you're right! I'm real stupid. I should have. That's right. It sure will. Yes, sir." Your elaborate politeness will drive your tormenter up the wall.

Or you can "play stupid." In a very serious tone of voice, fail to understand, and keep trying. "Oh, I see. The color of the paper is wrong . . . Oh, not the color . . . I don't understand . . ."

Even worse, agree—but then exaggerate your agreement beyond reason. "Hell, yes. I flunked out of here four months ago, and I still haven't found out." "I'm so stupid that when they set up a still life, I thought it was lunch and I ate it." No way to deal with that—incredibly effective!

Fogging is terrible for relationships; don't use it except as a last resort when you are on the ropes. And drop it as soon as the other person stops his offensive behavior.

Comment: With these tools you will be able to handle most people who try to put you down. It is not always a nice world out there. There are crazies walking around, and you must be confident that you can protect yourself. Therefore, it is a good idea to try these tools once or twice, before you put them away. And just once or twice. Being able to blow people away may give you a nice feeling of power. Don't go overboard with it.

One question that comes up frequently is, "Why should I admit I'm not a good person?" Because if, through desensitization, the statement, "You are a bad person" loses its emotional content for you, you will have achieved freedom. Every critical statement carries its clout only if you want the attacker to think you are a good person. Therefore most people spend a great deal of energy in denying the critical statement; and they defend, explain, and justify their actions. It doesn't work. It's a waste of time, effort, and energy to try to prove you are O.K. to a hostile, critical person. You can't do it. If, on the other hand, you agree at the beginning you are bad, *and it doesn't bother you to say so,* there is no further discussion, and you have lost nothing.

It might help to make a list of words that bother you. You might include such words as bad, lazy, stupid, or any other words that you would not like someone to use about you. Then repeat the words over and over, until they become meaningless for you.

Another question that comes up is, "Do I have to admit I did something wrong when I didn't? If someone says I am a thief, do I have to say "You're right, I am a thief, and I'm still a good person?"

In real life, of course not. But the choice has to be yours; it shouldn't just be a reflex denial. You have to be *able* to say it without raising your SUDS. So you have to *practice* admitting *anything* to your friends in the training situation. Then you can decide whether or not to say it in real life. You won't have to deny, just to reduce your SUDS by protecting your feeling of being a good person. You will know you're a good person anyway.

When you feel you have a handle on this, let your friends criticize everything you are sensitive about. You graduate and get your diploma from the criticism exercise when they can say *anything* to you without raising your SUDS. At that point you can listen carefully to their opinions, and either accept or reject them. You will be in charge of what to believe, and what seems untrue and useless. You will hear both, even from well-meaning people.

When your fear of criticism is under control, you can say, "Look, is there something going on I don't know about? Are you upset with me about something? If you are, I'd really like to know." Invite your friends to be straight with you. And when they are, listen, and don't "dexify."

You will surely suffer much criticism in your life. Now is the time to deal with it. When you can make peace with your own internal critics, and your self-esteem is secure, you can value criticism as the gift it often is. You will not only be happier, you will have better relationships, and you will do better work.

7 Confidence

Tracy became something of a celebrity in Iowa City when she won a Presidential Scholarship to Yale. At Yale she joined the select group that elected Directed Studies, an accelerated humanities-oriented program that combined small classes with eminent teachers. It was a program that attracted the brightest, most verbal, and most eager students, and for the first time Tracy really felt the pressure of competition. However, she kept up, did the work, and got her papers in on time, until, after about two months, she formed a disastrous relationship with an intensely religious, highly opinionated young man. He dominated her thinking and her life. On two occasions he hit her. As her relationship with him deteriorated, her academic work began to suffer, and her friends saw her confidence in herself begin to crumble. The combination was too much for her, and she dropped out.

Confidence is a Wonderful Feeling

When you have it, confidence is a wonderful state of mind. It is a safe and secure feeling, of effectiveness and invulnerability. You will have great friends, the ball will stick to your fingers, the teachers will admire your intelligence, the other sex will love you, and you will remain healthy forever. You know you will be able to deal effectively with whatever the world throws at you. The world is your pearl-filled oyster. Confidence is a unique feeling. But it is also not all that common among college students.

If you do have a basic sense of confidence, you are likely to have achieved it early in life. In the first chapter I described a child in a park who moves away from his mother, becomes anxious, returns for reassurance, and then goes off again. That time of life was important, because you made decisions then about the world that still influence your confidence level. If you knew mother was there in times of danger, you are more likely to believe that the world is basically safe, and to face it with confidence.

More important, however, as you grew up you learned

that even when the world is not all that safe, you can still handle it. You are capable of overcoming adversity. Confidence does not mean that things will always go well, but that you have learned to trust your ability to function well even when they go wrong. You have abilities and protections that are scaled to the adversity you encounter.

What are some of the things that can go wrong, and so undermine your confidence?

Tracy had made a relationship with someone whose background, ideas, and temperament were very different from hers, and when the relationship became strained she thought it was her fault. You may experience rejections by people you want to like you, and will wonder, "Is there something wrong with me?" In sports, you will at times miss shots, throw the ball to the wrong person, run the wrong way, lose contests you have worked hard to win, and hear the coach bellow, and other players laugh or groan. Sometimes as you look at homework you will not know what it means, and feel stupid. You will have compositions to write, and the white sheet of paper will be as blank as your mind. In class, you will sometimes not know the answers to questions while others discourse eloquently. Occasionally, your teachers may even be sarcastic.

For a while you are likely to find that your confidence has deserted you; that you are feeling anxious and insecure. This is almost inevitable. Sooner or later it happens to everyone in college. There will be black hours, when you experience despair and agonies of self-doubt. You may come to the conclusion that you are incompetent, inadequate, and worthless; that you will never be able to compete or win; that you don't have the "right stuff," and the sooner you drop out, the better.

Before you give yourself over to despair and helplessness, there are some things you can do to reduce your anxiety.

First, you do not need to add to its discomfort the false belief that you should not feel that way, or that there is something wrong with you if you do, or that you are the only one who does. Of *course* you are concerned about making it in college, and feel insecure. That's normal. Anyone would. Everyone does. Everyone in a new situation feels insecure. A loss of confidence doesn't mean there is something wrong with you, or that you are inadequate. Occasional feelings of insecurity are a normal, even necessary, part of growth. There is no way to approach a new or difficult situation without that feeling.

The first step to confidence, therefore, is to deal with the belief that you shouldn't ever lack confidence, or that feeling insecure means you are inadequate. Lack of confidence in a totally new situation is normal and reasonable. It is part of the learning process.

Then, take the time to think and remember. You have had these feelings before; how did you deal with them? Reflect upon your prior experiences in high school. You must have had similar feelings then, and eventually worked your way through or around them. Weren't there times when you experienced rejection by a person or a group, and believed for a time that you were hopeless, and yet went on to make good friends, even of those with whom you were having difficulty? Weren't there times when you did badly at sports, or in class, and yet eventually did well? Of course you felt confident at times. But you wouldn't be where you are now if you didn't have the ability to overcome adversity.

Ah, (you might say), but that was in high school. This

is college. True, but now you are older, and better able to deal with more difficult situations. As you grow, the problems grow with you, but your ability to find solutions to them grows, too. In fact, your personal growth needs problems that challenge you.

Life will always challenge you. I hope it never stops. And I hope you never stop growing to meet the challenge.

A loss of confidence in yourself, painful as it is, is temporary. Remember that you have had this feeling before, and that it went away. It might *feel* permanent, but it has always disappeared in the past, and it will disappear in the future. It is only a feeling, not a judgment, and like all feelings, will wax and wane. Stay with it, and, after a few good nights sleep and a few successes, you will feel confident again.

Another thing you can do is to re-evaluate your expectation of always doing things perfectly, or doing them well the first time. You may expect that things should come to you more easily than they do; and that if it is hard for you, you are untalented. But our reach should always exceed our grasp. Students often complain about the pace of some courses, in which there never seems enough time to learn it well. But it is perfectly all right to keep moving on into new areas before we have perfectly mastered the old. I think I first learned this from my violin teacher. Each week she would give me a selection to play, and instructions on how to play it. Each week I would play it clumsily, and she would say, "O.K., that's good, let's move on. This week, play selections . . ." When I would protest that I could play the prior week's selections much better if I spent another week practicing, she answered, "It's fine; and it will get even better in time. Don't beat it to death now. Let's go on." And almost against my will, I was week after week thrust into evergrowing complexity. It might have felt safer to stay with an area until I had gained mastery and felt competent, but she made me go on.

It may help you to remember that anything that is worth doing, is worth doing badly at first. As you stay with it, it will get better and better.

A good way to lose confidence is to compare yourself with students who can assimilate information more easily than you, are more verbal in class, and enjoy taking exams because they do so well. For most of us, however, good grades come with a lot of hard work. If you look around you at the people who are getting good grades, they are almost always the ones who are willing to make the commitment to work hard. No matter how quickly or slowly you learn, there is a certain amount of time you will have to put in to get good grades. How much time depends on you. But it will always be appreciable. Nothing of value comes easily. So it has less to do with "talent" than with your willingness to apply glue to the seat of your pants. Learning how to focus your attention on your work, hour after hour, is one of the most important skills you will learn at college. Complaints about talent or intelligence are usually a cop-out.

Sometimes the expectations that are hardest to deal with are those of your parents. Your parents' expectations are and should be important for you. You will want to fill them, and you might work very hard to do so, and that's good. However, you might think that your parents have expectations for you that are unrealistic, and that you cannot fill. For example, you might think they expect you to get a 4.0 average, and so feel discouraged. It may help a great deal if you talk with them about this. That they have expectations of you is good—that's a sign of their confidence in you—but sometimes expectations that are too high can be discouraging. Talk with them. Ask them what they expect of you. Get it out on the table. You may not have read them correctly. And if you honestly believe that their expectations are unrealistic, negotiate. See if they will still feel good about you if you only get a 3.0 average. Sometimes pressure is good; but often it helps to take some of the pressure off.

You may tie your self-esteem to your performance. But this is just too big a load for most of us to handle. Your job is difficult enough as it is without worrying about whether it is going to prove you are O.K. or not. It just adds too much unnecessary anxiety. A little anxiety improves performance, but too much anxiety sets you up for failure. If your self-worth is not tied to any specific success or failure, you will be less vulnerable to discouragement.

Don't Let Lack of Confidence Stop You

One of the most important things to learn is that you *can* function, and function well, even when you are not sure of yourself. The only thing to keep you from it is your own belief that you can't. It is great to find that you can function well even when you are not sure of yourself.

Look at good actors before a performance: they all feel anxious every time. Each performance is a new experience for them, and the insecurity gives them a degree of alertness and energy that adds to their performance. I have done a little acting, and I remember the trembling in the knees that afflicted me my first time on stage in front of an audience. I was saved from total stagefright by being able to let just enough of that tension into my voice when I needed it, and it gave more power to my words. An actor without anxiety before the curtain goes up will not give as good a performance. The anxiety adds luster and excitement.

The same is true of sports. A little anxiety adds that extra sense of awareness, of adrenalin, of power, that coaches look for in their stars.

Even in relationships, a little insecurity helps you be more aware of the other person's feelings and thoughts. You are less likely take the other person for granted. An overconfident person misses clues.

Another way to live with a temporary loss of confidence, and even use it to function better, is to call the feeling "excitement" or "anticipation" rather than insecurity or anxiety. It's the same feeling. Renaming it doesn't make it go away, of course, but it certainly can change how you look at it. People love the excitement of challenge; it would be a terribly uninteresting world without it. Excitement is the reason for roller coasters, downhill racing, and playing with fire. It is exactly the same feeling inside as insecurity, except that we have renamed it. Calling the situation challenging and exciting rather than dangerous makes it much easier to live with.

Insecurity is a sense of warning, that this is not a comfortable, old, well-worn situation; there are elements of newness, and you should be cautious and alert. You will do better if you heed that sense, but not let it immobilize you.

How Much Structure in Your Life Is Good?

One way to improve your sense of confidence is to increase the structure of your life. Lack of confidence is often the result of the anxiety of not knowing what to expect, and fearing the worst. Therefore structuring your life so that you have more control over it, and so know what to expect, can make you feel better.

Structure means being clear in your own mind about your objectives, your values, and your priorities, and ordering your life accordingly. This can range from a few ideas as to what life is all about, to the meticulous arranging of every moment.

Some schools and teachers will provide more structure than others. You may have classes that will give you specific reading assignments, tell you what you have to know, and test you on how well you have learned it. Others, however, will have less definite directions, and may depend more on you to organize the material and your time. Everyone needs some structure in their lives, but some more than others. Some students will flounder without a lot of structure, but do well once they or others have provided an outline for their lives. Other students need much less structure, and will chafe under too many constraints. You may have to experiment to find the right formula for you.

When you graduate, you will find a world out there that is less structured than college. Even in graduate school. Probably the most common and emotion-charged complaint I have heard from medical school students, for example, is that they no longer know what to study for exams. They now have to decide for themselves what and how much it is important for them to learn, and to take their lumps on exams when they guess wrong. They suddenly have to learn for themselves, in a new environment, with too much to learn, in not enough time, how to function without "enough" structure.

It is important to learn how to function when there is no or little external structure, and how to create your own structure, as necessary. No one will do it for you. Now is the time to learn how.

However, a word of caution. Too *much* structure can get in your way. You will, on balance, function more creatively if you don't need *excessive* structure. What is excessive structure? Compulsiveness is a good example of excessive structure. Compulsiveness means the need to know every last detail of a situation, to account for every second, to dot every *i* and cross every *t*. It means that you are being careful, not just because it is good for you, but because without it you may be overwhelmed by anxiety.

How can you tell if your structure is good, or compulsive? The best way is to experience being without it. If you can't tolerate being without structure because you get anxious, then you are probably being compulsive.

For example, imagine, if you will, being a "chip on the ocean." Sit in a comfortable easy chair, preferably with your legs up. Close your eyes and imagine yourself a chip of wood floating on the ocean. You have no way of controlling your movement or direction; you are at the mercy of the wind, the waves, and the tide. You are exposed to the elements; you experience the cold water, the sun, and rain. In the air are seagulls; in the water are plankton, fish, perhaps sharks. How do you feel? What do you do?

Most people enjoy the situation. They enjoy the sensation of not needing to have control. They "go with it."

They don't just do something, they lie back and relax. But others find this intensely uncomfortable, and must get out of this situation quickly by landing on a beach or by angrily stopping the fantasy. They have found this unstructured situation intolerable.

If you found yourself *needing* to do something to reduce the discomfort, you might want to ask your friends whether they see you as more compulsive than you need to be. If so, perhaps it would be a good idea to practice being less structured. You may find that if you do, the anxiety you feel at first may subside. If you find yourself needing to be compulsive just to reduce your anxiety, nip it in the bud now, before it owns you.

If you are either unable to structure your college life effectively, or, on the other hand, you can't help being compulsive, it is not a sign of weakness to ask for help at your counseling service.

Safe Courses—Safe Lives

Many students gravitate to undemanding classes that are mildly interesting, but do not require them to open their minds.

Courses that are beyond your present ability, and beyond your present ken, are the only courses that will lead to growth. New challenges are risky; they involve the possibility of failure. A big step into the unknown may even seem wrong to you if is beyond your experience. But isn't that what college is for? Steps that are too small and carry no risk leave you unchallenged.

Another way of not taking advantage of your college years is to limit yourself to "how-to" courses, and ignore the wide range of human experience that is presented in the humanities. Too specialized an education can sometimes give you the idea that there is a "right" way of doing things, and that you should know what it is. This idea is intimidating, and may inhibit you from experimenting with new ideas and different ways of doing things. A narrow vision leads to narrow behaviors.

There is a certain comfort in thinking that there is a right way of doing things, and that if you really learn the right way, you and the world will be all right. Unfortunately, the real world isn't at all like that. What worked yesterday may not work tomorrow. People who are attempting to maintain a "right way" (which they may see as a sense of order and reason) may find themselves being passed by, by events that cannot be ordered, and by less constrained people who find creative, ingenious, unpredictable solutions and avenues to the future. If change threatens us, in a world where change and originality are the lifeblood of creativity, attempts to resist change may cause stagnation and mediocrity.

To find creative solutions for your problems, you will have to have the confidence to occasionally *let go* of old concepts. This is sometimes amazingly difficult for people to do!

Rats in a maze will explore various pathways as part of their natural exploratory behavior. When they find food at the end of one particular path, they will learn to run directly to this path when they are hungry. If the food dispenser is then moved, they will resort to their exploratory behavior, again, until they find it. They will quickly learn to ignore the old path and run directly through the new to the food.

This is explained by the operant conditioning theory of

learning as a combination of extinction of the old behavior, and reinforcement of the new.

On the other hand, ethologist Konrad Lorenz in his book *King Solomon's Ring** describes a different kind of behavior in the water shrew. When he placed this small animal in a new caged environment, it cautiously and carefully created a path for itself, step by step. One such pathway led up a small hill to a rock and then to the level ground again. Once these animals were sure of their path, they would run up the hill, jump to the rock, jump to the ground, and then run on their way. One day, he removed the rock. The unsuspecting animal ran up the hill, jumped to the (missing) rock, and fell splat; picked itself up, and ran on its way. The next time, the animal again jumped to the missing rock, fell splat, picked itself up, and ran on its way. And, to the amazement of the ethologist, kept on repeating its fall, again, and again.

I sometimes think that humans have more in common with that small animal than with the rat. Once we have learned the "right" way of doing things, we tend to repeat that way, over and over, in spite of falling on our collective face again and again. We hold on to the old with feelings of pride and righteousness. When we are young, we learn new behaviors quickly. Unlearning them when they no longer work is much harder.

There is sadness, sometimes, in giving up old perceptions, and in seeing the world in a new way. We have resistance to doing this. Sometimes when we should give up an old perception, we hang on to it long after it is good for us.

In chapter I you did an exercise in which you said

* (New York: Harper and Row, 1979).

"Goodbye" to someone you felt you needed. Even harder is letting go of the way you have always done things. In order to cope well, you are going to have to say "Goodbye" to some old friends, your well-worn, time-tested ways of seeing the world, if you are to learn.

Sometimes people are so frightened by insecurity that they spend a lifetime erecting safe, secure situations for themselves. They immobilize themselves by rules of conduct and behavior, and by other symbolic representations of security. They are afraid to take risks. They take the apocryphal ancient Chinese curse, "May you have an interesting life" seriously. They become compulsive, rigid, bored, boring, and ultimately depressed.

What a dull world this would be, if it were always "safe!"

8 Motivation

You're sitting at your desk with books piled up on either side of you. You have at least three hours of studying to do. You've arranged your pens, opened your notebooks, and are ready to go. You start reading, and your mind wanders. You find that you've been looking at the same page for fifteen minutes, without knowing what you've been reading. You get up, get a glass of milk from the refrigerator, take a walk, talk to your roommate, and then go back to the desk. You bring your mind back to the subject, and it seems as dry and tasteless as a stale box of cereal. What's wrong? Is it you?

In this chapter, we will consider the subject matter, how it is taught, and how you study. We will discuss burn-out, emotional turmoil, and motivation.

Let's look at motivation first. Why are you studying? Why are you studying this particular subject? (Or not studying it?) Why are you at school in the first place?

The Career-Oriented Student

Career-oriented students know in advance why they are in school. They have a goal. They know what they want. They have already picked out a career for themselves, and they are already motivated. Their major problem is getting good enough grades to get into the graduate school of their choice.

Career-oriented students run into a real problem because of their need to get good grades for admission to graduate schools. This conflicts with the other needs of young adults. Students who live at the library and spend all their time working neglect many important aspects of college life. Many graduate students are socially inept, sexually naive, and emotionally close to burn-out.

Given the competitive nature of admission to good graduate schools, I don't know the answer to this. You will have to choose a path, and live with it. There is not always a "right" way to go, but I would urge you to live as full a college life as is consistent with the grades you need.

Gary's experience may be helpful to you. Gary wanted to be sure of getting into a good graduate school. Therefore he always mixed hard, career-oriented courses in which he needed a good grade with easier classes that he took just for fun, like an art class (which he took to satisfy his mother). When he needed a class for graduate school, he worked hard even when it wasn't enjoyable, because he was motivated; and when he took classes just for fun, he had such a good time he also got good grades. He took five years to go through college to ensure good grades and because he enjoyed himself so much.

He could see, he said, that many students who were as smart as he did not do as well because they sometimes took too many hard courses the same term.

The Intellectually Stimulated Group

And then there is the group that finds almost any subject intellectually stimulating. They like new ideas, and because there is a new idea on every page of their textbooks, they read them avidly, and are prepared for each class. They discuss philosophical ideas over lunch, and argue with the teachers.

They *enjoy* studying.

"Enjoy" is a strange word. It can have many shades of meaning. Let us define it as a sense of interest and pleasure.

I am not talking about "having fun." "Having fun" and enjoying what you are doing are not the same. Fun is something that appeals to the child in you who delights in games and sports and laughter.

When I say "the child in you," I am not putting that

down. The child in you is and will always be an important part of you, no matter how old you get. That fun-loving child in you adds spice and zest to life, and is the source of a great deal of creativity, in the arts, and in life in general. Don't ever lose it; the adult without an inner fun-loving child doesn't understand joy. I will talk more about it in the chapter on creativity.

But the child in you loves to be entertained, and the expectation of being entertained is inappropriate in college. Some classes are fun, and some teachers are entertaining, but if you think school *should* be that way, or that teachers who are not entertaining are boring, you have false expectations and you will be disappointed.

More important than fun is enjoying your work. Education can be very enjoyable. After all, the courses you are studying should be both new and interesting. They should stimulate your curiosity about how your world works. When you solve a problem or discover answers, especially to a question you didn't even know you had, you get a sense of satisfaction, even excitement, like no other experience.

When you are enjoying something, time passes quickly. The afternoon is gone before you know it. Also, when you enjoy doing something, you find yourself with more energy; you are less tired when you finish than when you started. Enjoyment of what you do energizes you. "If you want something accomplished, ask a busy person."

When you are enjoying what you do, you learn it almost effortlessly. You know what you have read, you marvel at it, it has become part of you. Does a baseball fan have to memorize the game's statistics to learn them?

Learning to *enjoy* your work, with an interest and excitement that comes from deep within you, is probably the most important thing you can learn in college. It will be a source of pleasure and stimulation for your whole life.

In Los Angeles UCLA sponsors the Plato Society, a society for retired people who still enjoy the discussion of ideas, and study for the pure pleasure of it. Their main focus is on weekly study classes, where sample topics include "The Life and Times of Montaigne" (conducted by a friend of mine), "The Labor Movement in the U.S. and Europe," and "The History of Peace and Related Treaties."

If you are such a person who studies for the sheer pleasure of studying, you are fortunate indeed. Still, the same word of warning I gave above to the careerist will apply to you also. Sometimes, such a love of learning can be instead of, rather than in addition to, a love of people. We all need the emotional growth that occurs when we talk about our feelings with other people who are talking about their feelings. It is not a good idea to intellectualize feelings; it cuts you off from them, in yourself and in others. That makes it difficult to understand people, and to make intimate relationships.

The "Is It Relevant?" Group

For others, a subject or a teacher must seem to be addressing them personally for the class to be interesting. Either a class "speaks to them," or it doesn't. When students say that a subject "doesn't have relevance," what they are saying is that it doesn't make contact with their own personal interests or experience.

For this group, to which I must admit I belong, a good

teacher is one who is interested both in his subject, and in *you*. A good teacher finds a way of making the connection between what you are learning, and you. The teacher you will remember fondly has this knack of making what he is teaching personal for you. Are you still fighting parental domination? Studies of oppressed people all over the world will have special meaning for you. Are you filled with feelings you don't understand? Psychology may ring a bell for you. Are you concerned with mortality or the meaning of life? You may find what you need in philosophy, or religious studies, or in pre-medical studies.

I remember a required course in classical civilization, my freshman year at college, in which I first learned about Athenian politics. We had a great lecturer, Eugene O'-Neill Jr., the son of the playwright, who made us aware that people then are much like us, and that civilization today is repeating on a large scale the same mistakes that caused the downfall of that small city-state. This personal and historical perspective was exciting for me. It tied in with, and perhaps stimulated, my interest in psychology, in which I later majored.

Many instructors do not know how to make their subject meaningful to you personally. They may teach a subject well, but not know how to relate it to the interests and background of the student. Sometimes the subject is taught only because it is "required," without your being able to understand *why* it is required.

In classes like this, you have a real problem, because unless you can discover the relevance of classes, and of education, for you, you may become bored and hostile. Educators know that it is much easier to learn material that adds to and amplifies your previous experience. They urge teachers to help you find the relationships between what you are learning, and what you already know. But not all teachers are educators. If you teacher can't help you, you may be able to help yourself by actively searching for some relevance to yourself, and to your experience. If you look hard enough, you may find the connection. But it will be up to you. Are you studying French? Plan a trip to France. My French teacher recommended a current French sexy novel. Does math leave you cold? Start a business and keep track of the money with a computer. *Make* yourself get involved. It's better than being bored.

External Rewards

Another reason for studying is the good feeling you get on hearing someone else approve of you, saying, "That was a good job." Such praise leads to a pleasant feeling of satisfaction and validation. We often work quite hard for that kind of external reinforcement. Praise from others whom we respect sometimes carries us quite a long way. We will sometimes study long and hard in order to receive this praise. And we will work for "tokens"; that is, grades. A good grade is a substitute for a teacher's verbal approval; and we enjoy getting it, and work for it. We even use it as currency to get more praise from our parents, and to feel good about ourselves.

Sometimes grades get to be more important than the course material. What will be on the exam becomes more important than what the course is about. Nothing takes the pleasure out of a course for a student more than worrying about the final exam. Nothing aggravates a teacher more, I think, than to wax lyrical about some wonder of life, and to have that inevitable hand come up with the question, "Do we have to know this for the exam?"

Certainly grades are important, not only for the career oriented, but also to use as feedback for how well you are doing compared to others. If you are getting low grades, you certainly will have to change your study habits. But please don't work *just* to get good grades; it interferes with enjoying what you are doing. It is difficult to work for grades and enjoy your subject, too. If you work because you are enjoying what you are doing, you will most likely also get praise enough, and good grades too. Let these external rewards be a side-product. Don't let your grades be the focus of your college life.

Internal reinforcement is much, much better. If we are to enjoy life, we must learn to depend on our own source of enjoyment that comes from within. Do *you* feel good about what you did? Did you feel good while you were doing it?

In an experiment, students were given three kinds of reinforcement. In the first group, the person was given praise, no matter what his level of achievement. In the second group, praise was given only for high achievement levels. In the third, the person was asked only, "How do you feel about what you did?"

Those in the third group scored highest in subsequent tests.

Why was this? In the first place, the first two groups were told in essence that someone else was in charge of deciding if their efforts were adequate. There is a part of us that dislikes such evaluation, even when the evaluation is good.

In addition, however, the third group was given the

opportunity to look at their own inner sources of satisfaction. In essence, they were asked to rely on their own feelings for reinforcement. The pleasure you give yourself is deep down yours. No one else can take it away.

If you enjoy what you are doing, if *you* are pleased with what you have done, and especially if in some way it touched you personally, you have become aware of one of the most powerful and satisfying pleasures there is in life.

You "Should" Study; It's Good for You

Another reason for studying, is that you "should."

Often you do something because it seems like a good idea. You certainly must think that college and even studying is a good idea. Certainly your parents think it is important. You probably realize it is in your (or possibly the world's) Long-Term Best Interests. Possibly you will have learned something important, and be a smarter person for it. You might even be a better person because of it. Besides, a lot of people are doing it, so it must be all right. It might even be something that will make you more money in the distant future.

Thinking about your Long-Term Best Interests may help you become better able to finish what you start, to think ahead, to take responsibility for your actions. Your LTBI may help you apply glue to your seat, even when you are bored with the material.

The sad truth, however, is that just because we know something is good for us, doesn't mean that we can do it. Will power and reason take us only just so far.

Besides, for many of us, what we "should" do makes us ill. What other people define as "good for us" creates a rebellious, opposite reaction.

"You should study more; you should eat better; you should exercise; you should finish this chapter tonight." It is strange how statements like that can make us squirm with discomfort. It is strange how hard it can be to do the things we "should" do. Why is it so hard?

There is a part of each of us that just hates to be told what to do. Once, when I told one of my children, age two, to stop playing and go to sleep, he replied defiantly, "You're not the boss of me!" And my young niece told her father, "You're always telling *me* what to do. When does it get to be *my* turn?" Life is a constant struggle between doing what other people say is good for us, and not doing it.

Learning to Enjoy Your Work

I think that as a parent I was no better than most; I wanted my children to work hard, and placed a great value on this. I became as frustrated and angry as most parents, when they did not fill my expectations, and communicated my disapproval to them. I think that two events saved us.

I used to clean up my yard every weekend. When the children became old enough, I assigned tasks to them. Then I yelled at them as they dawdled and delayed. It must have been very painful for everyone. One day my wife said to me, "Maybe you'll get more mileage out of them if you just tell them that we're all going to clean up the yard today, and ask them what each would like to do. They probably won't do what you would like them to do, but it might be more than they would do otherwise."

You know, it worked. Once I got over my preconceptions of how much and what they *should* do, they actually did quite a lot, and made play out of it, and enjoyed it. They *made play out of it!* Left to themselves, they made play out of work!!

If, now, you find yourself in the bind of not enjoying your work because play and work became an either-or dichotomy for you, perhaps you can redefine what work and play mean to you.

Resistance

At another time, I was beginning to believe that all my children were stupid. No matter how hard I tried to drill them in arithmetic or reading, it didn't seem that they they could learn or remember the simplest things. At a school conference, the teacher said, "You and they would be much better off if you didn't take the responsibility for what they learn. Let me motivate them, not you. If I can't make them *want* to learn, then your forcing them won't work either."

That was hard for me, but a relief, too. When I let go, they began to do better and better. They actually didn't hit their stride until college, when they approached their work with real enjoyment!

A lot of their difficulty had been their resistance to being pushed too fast too far too hard. Guidance is one thing; but pushing begets resistance, and resistance makes work very hard.

If you are stuck in a place where work is not fun, and even fun is not as much fun as it used to be, re-examine your resentment toward college work and teacher pressure. Almost certainly it is based on resistance to your parents' pressure. Perhaps you just have to back up a little. Your parents aren't here to push you any more, and your teachers in college generally won't. If you worked mainly because you were pushed, and if that external push doesn't exist anymore, then you may find it very difficult to work in college. When you were younger, you felt you needed to defend yourself against that kind of pressure. You don't need to any more.

One of the ways of not doing what other people want you to do is called "passive-aggressive resistance." "Passive-aggressive resistance" means you find ways of defeating the other person that are just short of being overtly aggressive. You just drag your heels, look stupid, show up late. You say, "What?" and "I just couldn't help it" and drive everyone else crazy. What is worse, you immobilize yourself.

Then when your inner voice says, "Study hard and get good grades," your attention wanders, you get restless, you can't concentrate, and you are suddenly hungry and have to go out for something to eat. Passive-aggressive resistance.

Procrastination

A special case of this is procrastination.

Rob says, "When I have to study, I get everything ready, and then I take a few minutes off, to talk, or to watch TV, and before I know, it's two hours later and I haven't done anything yet."

He calls home, and his mother asks, "Rob, have you finished your essay yet?" He replies, "I'm going to get to it right away . . ." Next week, she reminds him again, and he gets angry. "I know, I know; I will." "When?" "Soon . . ." Next week: "Have you done it yet?" "Don't bug me. I'll get to it." "When?" "Any day now."

Sooner or later, you really have to do these things. They *don't* go away. If you don't do them, terrible things may happen, and they're embarrassing. I don't think I want to tell you of some of the things I have been putting off doing. I keep a special file for these tasks. When I haven't done something I should for a week, I put them into a file marked "URGENT." When I haven't done them for a month, I put them into another file, marked, "MUST DO TODAY!" When I haven't done them for three months, I put them into another file I never look at.

Procrastination is caused by conflict within yourself. A part of you wants to do what has to be done, or you wouldn't have a problem; but there is another part, that really, really doesn't. It helps to say to yourself, "If I'm not doing what I think I really want to do, there must be a part of me that really doesn't want to do it. Let's look at it." Looking at that part of you can be hard, but it is worthwhile.

Rob has this little internalized voice of his mother always telling him what to do, and try as hard as he can, he can't do it. She isn't calling him on the phone; she is "inside" him, creating all kinds of guilt, but no action. That's simple passive-aggressive resistance.

On the other hand, you may be a "perfectionist"; that is, you are afraid of turning out something that is not up to some mythical standard, a common problem with people who procrastinate. It helps to remember, "Anything worth doing is worth doing badly." If it is important, you can always fix it up later. A word processor is wonderful for perfectionists; it gives them the opportunity to fix things up time after time after time. A word processor gives you the opportunity to rewrite a ten line paragraph fifteen times.

Perhaps you are afraid of failure. You might not get the approval or appreciation you would like; and the prospect of not succeeding freezes you before you even start. The antidote for this, for me, is to fantasize the worst that can happen . . . what is the worst that anyone can say about what I am about to do? Once I have put this into words, I can counter it with, "Well, it probably won't be *that* bad!" And that releases me, and I can start.

And, strange to say, there is even a part of some of us that is afraid of success. It may mean giving up ideas of helplessness, dependency, and being taken care of.

Whatever these voices, it helps to be able to "externalize" them. Put your mother in an imaginary chair, and have a conversation with her. Or put your "inner child" on your knee, and listen to what it has to say. Listen to what that part of you is trying to say. There has to be some voice inside of you that has a good reason for not doing what another part of you really wants to do. It has something to say to you. Don't ignore that voice; it won't go away. Give it a chance to be heard. After all, that voice is also you.

When you have seriously considered what that voice has to say, the rest of you, the adult part of you, has a chance to respond. Until then, you really don't have a choice. Knowing what you *should* do, can only take you so far, if you have another part of you blocking you.

Studying to Avoid Anxiety

The most common reason for studying is to avoid anxiety. It is also the worst reason in the world. It is the least rewarding and the most damaging.

A common scenario in college is that as exams approach, the anxiety level in the school rises. Many students say that until the anxiety level gets high enough, they can't make themselves study. Anxiety can get so thick you can almost touch it. You may look disheveled, tired and unsmiling. You may get short-tempered and irritable. Competitiveness turns nasty, and tempers flare. Liquor flows (just to help relax, of course), and lights burn until two A.M.

What is that all about? Is it necessary? Is it good for you?

Many people, both students and instructors, seem to think so. Their thinking goes something like this. Anxiety is seen as a sort of whip to make you perform better. If you aren't anxious you won't study enough. If you get anxious enough, you will study harder and will do well on the exams; therefore, if you don't feel anxious enough, you have to create anxiety. The teachers who can create the most anxiety have the students with the best scholastic records. Since students are accustomed to using anxiety as a reason for studying, lowering anxiety would eliminate studying.

What is sad, of course, is that to some extent this is all true. Is that what college is about? I don't think so. I hope not.

To begin with, anxiety and enjoyment are not compatible. Anxiety is a terrible feeling. You can't enjoy studying if you are also anxious. If you are anxious, you can't enjoy the subject you are studying and you probably won't enjoy college. Interest and enjoyment are, in the long run, far better reasons for studying.

Besides, studying to relieve anxiety has an important built-in "self-destruct" aspect. When anxiety is attached to studying, studying becomes *unpleasant.* That's basic psychology. If we study only when we are anxious, we won't like studying and we will have difficulty getting ourselves to study.

Students who rely on anxiety to motivate themselves to study often never open another book after college. They've "done their studying," they didn't like it, and they won't do it again.

Furthermore, a life built on avoiding anxiety does not have long-term prospects of happiness. Anxiety may get the immediate job done, but it is a temporary victory; the anxiety will still be waiting for you around the corner, not just before the next exam, but all your life. Students who study to avoid anxiety never learn the joy of learning or of living.

As, however, your anxiety recedes and is replaced by interest and enjoyment in your subjects, college and life will become a much more satisfying and fulfilling experience for you.

B. F. Skinner, the psychologist who is the father of operant conditioning, noted that people will learn either to get good feelings, or to avoid bad ones. After years of studying this phenomenon, he came to the conclusion that negative conditioning (that is learning in order to avoid bad feelings), should not be used in schools, because it was bad for the students, emotionally and intellectually. In the long run it is bad for the learning process, the schools, and society itself.

Perhaps, when you are educators, you may be able to

change the system. For now it is more important for you to learn for yourself how to cope with college-related anxiety.

I will talk more about anxiety and what to do about it later; it deserves a chapter by itself.

Study Habits

In the pressure of adjusting to college, a new term, or a new course, it is easy to fall behind, and hard to catch up. If this happens to you, you will understandably not like the experience. It is hard to like a class where you don't know what's going on because you're two weeks behind.

Sometimes it is just a matter of time. Time management is like a budget; too much time spent in one place often leaves you without enough time for another. A budget is important for your finances, and a time management budget is important for your time needs. It is a a good idea to establish priorities for yourself, budget your time accordingly, write it out in a chart. Then, when you would like to spend time on your social activities, or money on a new gadget, you can look at your budget and see if you can afford it. And after you have made your budgets, stick to them.

Time can either be your enemy, or your friend. To make time your friend, you must not take it for granted. If you don't take care of it, it won't be there when you need it. At the beginning of the year, you may think, "I've got a whole year to get the work done." When you have six months left, you may say, "No rush, I still have six months." When you have three months left, you say, "I have to get to work." Then when there is only a month left, you say, "Where did the time go? I haven't enough time!" The last week, you say, "They give us too much work. I can't do it all! I'm no good."

That's no way to treat a friend.

If you make a game plan, spend enough time each day on your work, leave time for your friends, recreation, and exercise, and go to sleep at a reasonable hour every night, time will be a good friend to you. You will know you have the time to accomplish what you need to do, and be confident of your ability.

One aid I have found invaluable is a notebook, the kind known as an "organizer." In the calendar portion, you might keep your regularly scheduled classes and assignments. Then you might add any extra assignments or appointments that come up. A weekly calendar works out well for me.

In addition, I make two lists. On one, I write everything else I have to do or buy this week. I add these as they come up, or as I think about them. I must be compulsive about this, because otherwise I forget. When I have taken care of them, I cross them out. Then, every week, I transfer everything left over to a second list, throw away the first list, and start that one over on another page. This way, every day I am reminded of what I have to do, and what I am putting off; and I avoid the "out-of-sight, out-of-mind" trap that would leave me with unpleasant surprises, and "I forgot" excuses.

Sometimes, getting behind has to do with *how* you study. When, in spite of studying hard, you still can't understand or learn the material, some counseling from an educational specialist may help. Sometimes it can be a simple matter of learning to organize the material, or of understanding what the teacher wants. Often students try to learn too much and get lost in detail.

Also, many students have "learning disabilities," which is a bad name for not organizing thoughts the way others do. Some people need to spend more time than others to make sense out of our language, either written or spoken. They often feel more comfortable with pictures, can't spell, and find it hard to read textbooks or to make sense out of lectures. It is not unusual; a researcher at Johns Hopkins says that almost 50 percent of all people tested need special attention in one area or another.

Julie concluded early in her life that she was just dumb. Much of what she read just didn't make sense to her. She got bad grades in public school from teachers who didn't understand why she didn't understand. She told her parents that she was "wired wrong." She was already in high school before her parents paid attention, and had her tested by a psychologist. He found that she was "dyslexic," which means that she reversed letters and so had difficulty understanding certain words. She went to a special school for a year, in which she learned how to pay attention to words that were difficult for her. When she learned to do this, she began getting good grades, and did just fine in college. She had always been bright; but she just hadn't been performing well. Many people of accomplishment including Picasso and Nelson Rockefeller were dyslexic.

Burn-Out

People who write about burn-out usually are talking about adults in high-stress jobs. But I think burn-out clearly shows itself in college. It is present even in young children, who stop trying in school because of an unrealistic sense of inadequacy. Burn-out occurs when your efforts to achieve your goal exceed your physical and emotional capability for a prolonged period of time. Everyone can work hard, and even work above their heads for a while, if they have enough time to recover. Without enough recovery time or when emotional factors interfere, you begin to burn out. And even if you achieve your goals, burn-out begins when you feel the effort or the achievement "wasn't good enough!"

Working hard, learning, and becoming proficient and technically skilled, is good for your career, and for your self-esteem. You must certainly not be content with mediocrity and sloppiness, or pleased with yourself in spite of inadequate standards. Competence is an important part of self-esteem.

On the other hand, how competent must you be? Most people I know have adopted a false standard of competence: superiority. This can be carried to ridiculous extremes in both directions. I listened to a student who was depressed because she only got an A- on a test; previously she had a 4.0 average. (For once I didn't know what to say.) Our country idolizes young people who get perfect scores in the Olympics. What kind of crazy message does that give all the other young people? A fifty-year-old ex-athlete gives an interview in which he says that the greatest tragedy in his life was coming in second in an Olympic event. In June 1986, a young woman who was losing a marathon race jumped off a bridge and became paralyzed. What about the rest of us? Must we all forever feel like failures because we didn't finish first?

What Comes Easy May Be Best

How important is it to stay with classes that might be important for your future well-being, but which turn out to be uninteresting and uninspiring? It is really hard to know when you should stick things out, and when you should cut your losses and run. On one hand, there is some advantage to learning how to persevere through adversity. On the other hand, suffering for the sake of suffering is a virtue that can be overdone. Sometimes sticking things out is a mistake.

Sometimes what you like doing, and what comes easy for you, may be precisely what you *should* be doing! Not enjoying what you are doing is sometimes an excellent reason for not doing it. Perhaps it would be better to take subjects you enjoy more. You may find that you really enjoy psychology, physics, art, philosophy, or history. Well, why not? You will probably do well in the courses you enjoy the most. Success begets success, and failure begets failure. If you find you are doing well in some unexpected field, maybe that is a message to you that you should change your goals.

We sometimes are burdened by a puritanical feeling that what we enjoy is somehow not valuable; that what is valuable is not pleasurable. Our internal critics tell us that there is something wrong if we are not suffering enough. Knowing when to take the easy route, and when to "hang in there," requires judgment, soul-searching self-knowledge, advice, help, and counseling. It is really hard making these choices. Just remember, that there is never a "bad" way to go, just many different paths, all of which curve around bends so that it is hard to see where they are going to lead.

In order to better understand the difference between working because you enjoy what you are doing, and working for grades, try the following exercise.

EXERCISE 12. Clay and Process

Purpose: To understand enjoying the PROCESS.

Method: Put a piece of clay the size of your fist in front of you, and then blindfold yourself. Make sure you cannot see what you are doing. Start mashing the clay, squeezing it, moulding it. Create an object. When you are through, destroy the object *before* you take off the blindfold. Do *not* look at what you have done.

Comment: Painful, wasn't it? You really wanted to look at what you had done, didn't you? That is understandable; you wanted to see what it looked like. And also, you wanted to know how *well* you had done, not only in your own eyes, but in the eyes of anyone else who might be there.

Now I want you to repeat this experience, over and over, until you discover the feeling of enjoyment you can get just in the feel of the clay as you mould it, just in the sensation of squeezing it and smoothing it, just in the *process* itself, rather than in the product. When you have arrived at the point where you are enjoying the process, the product will also be more satisfying to you.

9 Coping with Bad Feelings

As they put the coffee on and the toast down, Shirley's roommates asked, "How was your date last night? Whatsisname? Johnny?"

"Oh, fine."

"So what happened?"

"I don't want to talk about it."

The roommates exchanged glances. "Come on, Shirl. Tell us. What happened?"

Shirley struggled for a few minutes to maintain her composure. Then she put her head down on her hands, and began to cry. One of her roommates put her arms around her, while sobs shook her body. The other stroked her hair, and murmured, "Go ahead. It's O.K. Get it out."

In a few minutes the sobs subsided. Shirley wiped her eyes, blew her nose, and said, "It was awful. I thought he liked me. I really liked him. We've been going everywhere for the past month. And then last night we went to the Chi Phi party, and he started dancing with this awful looking pink-haired bitch, and then he didn't pay any more attention to me . . . I felt just awful. I was so ashamed and embarrassed . . . and then I got really angry . . . I told him I was leaving, and he just didn't care. I felt so alone, so bad, I thought I would die. I mean I really thought about dying!"

Micki said, "Oh, Shirley, you must feel so awful. I'm sorry."

Millie said, "Oh, Shirley, you shouldn't feel that way; he wasn't worth it. Don't waste your tears." And began buttering her toast.

Shame, embarrassment, anger, loneliness . . . and then, to make it worse, Millie telling her she "shouldn't feel that way."

We often hear that message, "You shouldn't feel that way." Of course, no one likes to feel bad. But although feelings may be painful, we must not deny or try to avoid them, only to deal with them. We must learn to live with them, not to flee from them.

Millie also tried being logical: "He wasn't worth it." She probably meant to be helpful, but logic just doesn't work well when feelings take over. Giving people logical reasons why they shouldn't feel they way they do may shut them up, but usually doesn't change their feeling. They just won't tell *you* about it again.

There is another message we hear constantly, that we

should be happy, all the time; that if we are not, there is something wrong. Buy these clothes, take this vacation, drink this beer, and you will achieve happiness. Indeed, we have available to us a wide range of medications and drugs so that we don't have to feel unhappy. Uppers, downers, tranquilizers, sedatives, alcohol, mood-alterers, mind-benders, psychedelics, narcotics; drugs to make us "happy" and "feel better" can be taken into every orifice. And all so that we don't have to feel unhappy.

The problem is, that if we take drugs to feel better, we never learn to cope with pain. And life is full of pain. It may feel very bad, but it won't kill us. We have to learn to handle pain, and not be blown away. We must learn to experience sadness, and go on; to feel hurt, anger, humiliation, and all the other feelings we are going to feel, and still be there tomorrow.

Furthermore, our feelings are not up for evaluation. If we are to accept ourselves as we are, we must accept our feelings as they are. When we are ashamed of feeling ashamed, embarrassed to be embarrassed, or afraid of being afraid, then we find living itself more difficult.

That doesn't mean that our feelings won't change; of course, they will. And it certainly doesn't mean that we have to act on them! We are not in charge of what feelings arise in us; but we are certainly in charge of what we do about them. What to do about these feelings, especially negative feelings, is what coping is about.

It may be hard to believe when you are feeling bad, but even *terrible feelings subside when you express, share, and then fully explore them.* And that is a necessary first step to understanding and then ultimately dealing with them.

Feelings will surprise you by becoming less painful and

less controlling if you 1) allow yourself to feel these feelings at their worst for as long as it takes, 2) share them
with others, and then 3) explore and understand them.

A Few General Rules

Here are some general rules for coping with uncomfortable feelings.

1. Accept your feelings as normal, natural, and worthwhile. Don't fight the feeling as though it were somehow
wrong to have it. If you're "hooked" (i.e., if you agree
with your inner critic that you're terrible), don't thrash
around like a fish struggling against the line; just lie there
and examine the hook. Are you really terrible?

Don't run away from the feeling. Don't take *anything*
into you (liquor, pills) to reduce the feeling. Don't attack
someone. And don't make a joke of it.

2. Find someone to talk to about that feeling. Share it.
Get it out in the open. Put it into words: "I had this
feeling . . ." As you talk, don't generalize; be specific.
Describe exactly what happened. What was the situation?
Describe it in great detail. Who said what? Who did what?
Then what happened? What did you do? Describe the
place, the people, how people looked, what they were
wearing, the whole environment.

Get in touch with the actual feeling itself. What was it?
Shirley said, "I had this terrible feeling of embarrassment,
and shame. Then, I felt lonely." And don't just talk about
the feeling, re-experience it. What was it like for you?
What was the actual bodily sensation you were experiencing? If you feel like crying, let it happen; it's O.K. to cry.
If you find yourself getting angry or scared, get angry or

scared. And stay with the feeling for as long as it takes to subside.

To fully experience a bad feeling often takes help. It is hard to do by yourself. We are too easily deterred by the pain, or trapped into pockets of anger, blame, self-pity, and gloom. To fully explore feelings, we need to be able to talk about them, with another person. So no matter how much it hurts, or how embarrassing it may be, put your mouth in gear, and *talk.* We have to be able to say what happened and how we feel, to be able to deal with our feelings. Otherwise we go around and around, stuck in one groove, unable to get unstuck.

Good friends can really help, sometimes, just by listening while we reach our own conclusions. Sometimes friends, no matter how good, are not enough to get us unstuck. Then, it is worth visiting a trained counselor, who will not only listen, but can also help guide you to your own resolutions.

3. Then, explore the *meaning* that feeling has for you. Find out what the feeling is saying about you, and face it. Remember what you were thinking, all the thoughts that were going through your head. Get them all out into the open. How long have you had such feelings? How did they start? Is one of your basic needs being frustrated? What's the problem, really? *What were your conclusions* about people, about yourself, and about the world? Perhaps Shirley had been insecure about her ability to attract men since her father walked out on his family when she was eleven.

Feelings may be the natural result of your experiences and the conclusions you drew about them, beginning at a very early age. Allowing, understanding, and accepting your feelings make them less painful in the long run, and more important, less controlling. You need not fight them, run away from them, or give in to them. They may become, instead, an important part of you, and an important part of your learning experience.

Furthermore, you now have the opportunity to re-examine conclusions you reached at a very young age, in a different context; conclusions which, although no longer valid, may still be influencing your whole life.

Most important, however, you may find out more about yourself—your own needs, wants, and desires.

Glad, Sad, Mad, or Scared

Feelings are very complex. Grouping them may help you get a handle on them in yourself. The simplest grouping is that of *glad, sad, mad,* or *scared.*

Relate these feelings to your needs. When your needs are met you feel "glad"; you have good, warm feelings about yourself and the world. When you fear they won't be met, you feel "scared." When you have feelings of frustration, and blame those "responsible," you become "mad": angry at the world, the situation or the other person. When you accept that your need is not going to be met, at least for now, you become "sad."

Thus, when Shirley was getting ready for the evening, she looked at herself in the mirror, and liked what she saw and she felt "glad": pleased, proud, self-assured.

She believed she had made a connection with a wonderful person, so "glad" also meant that she felt loved and loving, accepted and accepting, valued and belonging.

When her friend began paying attention to someone else, she found herself "scared," because she feared being abandoned. She also felt "mad"; angry that he made her feel that way.

But she ended up feeling "sad": she felt ashamed, embarrassed, inadequate and unattractive. She also had feelings of loneliness, hopelessness and abandonment, and wondered if life was worth living. She was depressed.

What can Shirley do about all this? She has experienced her feelings fully, ventilated them thoroughly, and shared them with her roommates. She feels heard and understood. She is still lonely, angry, and depressed, but she feels better. Why must she do anything? What's wrong with her feeling what she feels?

There is *nothing* wrong with having these feelings. Feelings aren't right or wrong. It is perfectly all right to stop here, and continue to be lonely, angry and depressed.

But there is quite a lot she *can* do, if she wishes. She can use her feelings as messages to herself, about her ability to fill her own needs, and her conclusions about who is in charge of her happiness. And she can then act on those messages.

What Can You *Do* with These Feelings?

You have gotten in touch with your feelings, shared them, understood them as best you can.

1. Now, ask yourself, what feeling would you *like* to have? How would you *like* to feel? The old feeling, caused by what happened, made you feel a certain way. Can you imagine the opposite? For example, Shirley might imagine how it would feel to be loved and admired by someone she loved.

2. If you can do that, then ask yourself, how could that happen? What would you really like to happen in your life? What is the best thing that could possibly happen to you? Shirley might imagine Johnny groveling, begging to be forgiven and taken back, and making him suffer while she spurns him until, as the beloved homecoming queen, she grandly forgives him but goes off with her new lover. Hearts and flowers. Fadeout.

Imagine your fantasy in great detail, and in all its dimensions. Don't be too practical; and don't be too specific. Just let your fantasy take you to a better place.

Don't narrow your horizon too much. People can believe that there is only one way to get somewhere. Shirley could, for example, complain that all she wanted was her Johnny back; now that Johnny has disappeared from her life she has no further chance of happiness; there will never be anyone else who can give her the same feelings of happiness; she is doomed to an empty, lonely, loveless life. And she may believe this so strongly that she is immobilized.

After a while, of course, we begin to realize that there will be other relationships, other chances of happiness. When you are feeling unhappy, you may not even want to think about that. But it is in your power to fantasize how you want it to be. It may not be entirely realistic, but it doesn't hurt to *imagine* other ways of getting your needs met.

3. If you are successful, this lets you get in touch with the feeling you would have, if that fantasy really happened. Of course it won't happen, but what would that feeling be like, if it did? What would it do for you? How would you feel if your fantasy really came to pass? Stay in touch with that feeling. You can see how this can reinforce your good feelings, in step 1. This is a nice way of breaking a self-destructive, vicious circle.

4. At the same time, however, you are going to have to let go of the old image of happiness you used to have, and this may require some active grieving on your part. You are going to have to say, in one form or another, "Goodbye, my previous route to happiness."

"But," you might say, "I don't *want* to say goodbye! That's the problem! I want my happiness back." Of course. But you have to say "Goodbye" to *that route* to happiness. You know by now that life is not all going to be easy. Well, you just had another lesson. What you are saying goodbye to, and grieving for, is the easy route to happiness. What you are saying goodbye to, is illusion. Johnny was *not* the best route to happiness. And doing your grieving for old ways is necessary for finding new ways.

5. Once you have talked, and explored, and grieved enough, it is time to go on to the next step. You have identified how you want to feel, and you have explored in your own mind various fantasies that might lead to that feeling. Now you have to *make decisions,* and to *act* upon them.

Daydreams and fantasies are how people explore possibilities. Then you have two choices. You can wait to see what, if anything, will happen. Or you can go out and *make* something happen.

You Can Just Wait

In general, if you wait long enough for something to happen, it won't. What generally happens is nothing. The "cute meet," contrived by a generation of script writers, has become part of our culture. If you stare long enough at a picture in the museum, someone is supposed to trip into you, and then ask you for your telephone number. Most likely, however, it will be the guard telling you that it's closing time.

Of course, sometimes things do have a way of working themselves out, and this often takes time; it may not happen suddenly. A little patience sometimes pays off. A way of expressing this is to say, "Don't push the river." Personally, after a while, I tend to take out my oars and give the river a little push.

Give up the expectation that you can sit in your room and that people will knock on your door to fill your needs. It may happen, but you are more likely to fill your needs by going out and *doing* something about it. That means making yourself available and friendly, being authentic and caring, and learning to respond appropriately. Put yourself out there where the action is; the more social interactions you have, the more likely you will fill your needs.

Now, let us look at a common feeling that seems to make all this impossible: shyness.

Shyness

Shyness is a terrible feeling. You can't start a normal conversation with others, and you respond to their overtures with humiliating embarrassment. You feel like a blundering, incompetent, inadequate fool. Everyone on campus knows about and laughs at you. You withdraw to your room in agonies of despair. Your fear of rejection is immobilizing. Shyness is one of the most anguishing disabilities known.

You can deal with shyness using the steps I described above. Allow your awful feeling to be; don't push it down. You probably know someone with whom you are not shy, and to whom you can talk about the situation. If so, share your thoughts, your conclusions, and your feelings. Even if you have to do it by yourself, take the time to explore your feelings thoroughly. How long have you had them? How did they start? Then imagine how you would like to feel, and fantasize what you would like to happen, and how that would make you feel. Decide what you are going to do about it, and then practice doing it.

With shyness, practice is especially important. Don't start by tackling the most difficult situation. Begin by role-playing with a friend. Role-playing is very good at making you comfortable with what you want to say. Say it over and over! Three key words in getting good at anything are practice, practice and practice. Practice means that you start out awkward and end up skilled. Making friends is a skill. Don't expect to be as skilled at first as you will be later. Don't judge yourself by your first clumsy efforts.

Then, talk to someone relatively easy to talk to, someone not likely to give you a hard time. Stay with easy situations until you have a little more confidence. Finally, when you feel ready, take the plunge. Don't put it off forever.

Perhaps the most practical advice I can give you is to go out there and practice getting rejected. Does that sound weird to you? *Practice getting rejected?* Why inflict such pain on yourself? Because unless you do it, over and over again, the fear of rejection will never go away! It will always haunt you, and influence your decisions all your life. If, on the other hand, you let yourself experience it over and over again, in gradually increasing doses, it will become easier and easier. Use the SUDS table (see Chapter V). Translate the feeling into a number, and watch the number get smaller. Eventually your SUDS will subside to the point where they become quite manageable. As they do, the challenge will become more interesting, and eventually, even fun. At that point you will be more assertive, less shy, and much more likely to have an impact on your world and get what you want for yourself.

Some Self-Destructive Ways Of Dealing With Feelings.

Since everyone has painful feelings, perhaps you should take a good look at your present ways of handling them. Do your present ways work for you?

Denial and Suppression

The most common way of handling bad feelings is to deny them, push them down, suppress them. I have a poster in my kitchen that says, "The only thing worse than not expressing your feelings is not knowing what they are."

Make A Joke About Your Feelings

Another way of avoiding uncomfortable feelings is to make a joke about the situation or yourself. Sometimes jokes about painful feelings help cut them down to size and make them easier to handle. But jokes at your expense, or at the expense of your feelings, make your feelings seem not worthwhile. Your feelings *are* worthwhile, and are *not* to be trifled with.

Common wisdom holds that comics are often very sad people who try to protect themselves by cracking funny jokes. Woody Allen has become a folk hero by exploring sensitive issues with which people are uncomfortable. His humor reveals even more about his own internal conflicts and unhappiness.

Attack

Attacking others is another common way to reduce uncomfortable feelings. It is so easy to believe that uncomfortable feelings come from "out there," that if only the other person were better, or the situation were better, you wouldn't feel uncomfortable; ergo, they are to *blame!* Attacking people may make you feel better, and sometimes gets you some limited goals. However, it destroys relationships. People will avoid you if you frequently attack. If you want good relationships, don't blame others for how you feel.

Compulsions

Compulsiveness is another way of avoiding anxiety or uncomfortable feelings. Compulsiveness means needing to do things a certain way, or have things in a certain order, in order to feel O.K. For compulsive people, even the slightest obstacle or delay can cause terrible feelings.

As long as what they are doing "works," they may not even know they have a compulsion.

You probably know some people who not only keep their rooms neat, tidy, and under control—which is fine—but who get hysterical if you dent a pillow on their couch. And then they think *you're* the one who is strange.

"Security blankets" are a mild form of compulsion. You may remember Linus, in the comic strip "Peanuts," who keeps a "security blanket" handy. You may even know some child with such a blanket that he keeps within reach, and fingers every once in a while. It is sometimes called a "boo." As long as his "boo" is available, such a child is perfectly normal. Take his "boo" away and you will see an exhibition of hysterical rage that will shock you. Parents don't mess with this; they make sure the "boo" is handy.

Addictions

If the "boo" is ingested in some way, the compulsion is called an addiction. There is no real difference between a compulsion and an addiction. Cigarette smoking, for example, is an addiction. As long as a cigarette smoker has a pack of cigarettes available, he feels perfectly normal. Remove that pack of cigarettes for a day, and the cigarette smoker will go berserk! Restore his cigarettes, and the smoker, after a few deep drags, will relax, and agree that, yes, it is a terrible habit and some day he will stop.

Almost anything can be or become an addiction. The most common and serious addictions in this country are to alcohol, drugs, and food. People who are addicted often talk as if the chemical dependency were all there is to it, but there is a very important psychological aspect to addiction.

Don't Use *Anything To Feel Better*

I raised three teenagers who were exposed to the drug scene, yet survived and thrived. I like to think that advice I gave them was of some help. I suggested: don't use *anything* in order to make you feel *better* when you are feeling *bad.*

Let's say you are going to a party where everyone is drinking beer, or smoking marijuana. If you are feeling good, having a good time, and enjoying the party, let your conscience be your guide. But if you are feeling uncomfortable or awkward, don't use the alcohol or drugs in order to feel better. Don't use them in order to reduce anxiety about being "accepted." Wait until you feel better and are enjoying yourself before you put anything in your mouth. There are too many times in life when you will feel bad, and these things, like crutches, work too well in temporarily reducing emotional discomfort. If you use these crutches to feel better, you stand a good chance of "needing" them, and becoming emotionally dependent. Emotional dependence is a major part of drug, alcohol, and other addictions.

You need to learn how to handle bad feelings; you don't need to reduce them with alcohol or drugs. Using alcohol or drugs to relieve bad feelings is the best way to get hooked on these substances which can control and ultimately destroy your life.

Food, Too!

You may be surprised to find food included here. Food is a more socially accepted way of reducing anxiety. It has the same magical property of making you feel better when you are tense or depressed.

Food is an easy addiction to pick up because many mothers use food as a tranquilizer. When a baby cries, a bottle often gets stuck in its mouth. Later, when mothers are anxious, they often make food a battleground with their children. You know, "Clean the plate, they're starving in . . ." So I am not talking about food to relieve hunger, but about food to relieve anxiety. Anxiety can cause a discomfort in the stomach that feels like hunger, and food relieves both. Since people can't tell the difference, they eat when they are anxious, even when they are not hungry. We've all seen people who are compulsive eaters.

Another serious problem related to food is that of anorexia nervosa, and bulemia. Anorexia nervosa is a condition in which people, usually young women, believe they must eat less, even when they are gradually starving to death. Bulemia is a condition in which they regularly binge on food, and then make themselves throw it up. As many as 20 percent of the women at one eastern college were identified as suffering from one or the other. One of them said to me, "When I was growing up, food was the only thing that lay completely within my control. And at first I was a little overweight, and I went on my first diet when I was nine, and then my mother thought that was just great. Besides, it showed me I had a lot of will power. When I was 13, I was 5'1" and weighed 85 pounds. My doctor told me if I kept it up, I would get very sick. My parents took me to a psychologist. It took me a year to get back to a normal weight. Whenever I get into any kind of trouble, my first impulse still is to stop eating. It makes me feel better."

Even if you yourself are not involved, if you see women who are regularly not eating, or who, after eating, go into the bathroom to vomit, please do not turn away from them. They need help. They can die from this. It is your business to tell someone who can help. Don't leave it up to the person concerned; if they could do anything about it by themselves, they would. If you see it, it becomes your responsibility to your fellow-student.

If You Are Already Addicted

Getting unaddicted is much harder than avoiding addiction. Few can do it by themselves; almost everyone needs help. I have a young cousin who was addicted to drugs while in high school, and led a marginal kind of life, personally and scholastically. He changed schools several times, finally making it into college, but then failed every course but one. At that point he went for help, and entered a drug rehabilitation program. His college, with a very good attitude toward recovered (or recovering) addicts, accepted him back, gave him credit for the one course he had passed, cancelled out all his previous grades, and gave him a fresh start. He responded with four A's and a B+. What a difference that rehabilitation program meant to his life! He is still "recovering" rather than recovered because his life, like everyone else's, has its full measure of stress, problems, and unhappiness, and he is tempted over and over to turn to drugs to relieve his feelings.

If you are addicted, stop denying, stop rationalizing, stop procrastinating. If you are willing to kick the habit, and if you have tried by yourself and failed, don't fool around any more. Call your counseling service and get professional help.

10 Anxiety

Lauren, a chemistry major, is a top student in college. Before every exam she calls home, cries, tells her parents she hasn't been able to study enough, and is afraid she is going to flunk. After every exam, she calls again and blithely announces she got another A.

We use the word fear about things that are real, and can harm us. If a berserk bull elephant is charging down the street at us, we feel fear. As with anger, our hearts pump faster and harder, we run faster, we jump higher, but with fear we are oriented to flight, not fight.

What Lauren is experiencing, however, isn't fear, it's anxiety. Anxiety refers to much the same sensation, but it has less to do with real events, than about our past experiences, and our thoughts and feelings about those events. If you are concerned about elephants in college, you are probably experiencing anxiety.

When Lauren tells her parents that she has not studied enough, is going to flunk, and won't get the grades she needs for graduate school, they must believe that this is legitimate fear. But when this happens again and again, and she reports A's on exams, they must re-evaluate and conclude that their daughter is subject to anxiety attacks. What, they will ask, was that all about?

What is anxiety all about? What causes it?

Anxiety
Anticipates Awful Consequences

Like fear, anxiety anticipates consequences. Unlike fear, these consequences have less to do with reality than with your own personal interpretation of those consequences. Anxiety depends to a great extent on how good, or how bad, your past experiences were, and what your conclusions were about them. We may have left over within us from early days fears of abandonment or physical abuse or death based on events that were or seemed real enough then, but are not real anymore. Or we all surely have left over some early feelings of guilt, shame, embarrassment, humiliation, and low self-esteem. The fear and anticipation of these feelings happening now is felt as anxiety.

The consequences of some situation may not seem so terrible to someone else, but if you are anxious, they seem terrible to you. After all, no one else has had your experiences, so no one else can tell you that you "shouldn't" feel anxious. So when someone is anxious about some future event, I ask, "Well, if this did indeed happen, what would that mean for you?"

For example, I said in Chapter I that we all need nurturing; it is a basic, human need for which we depend at first on our family and friends. When you came to college, these pathways were gone, and you probably became homesick. But you then developed other pathways to feeling nurtured; you developed other relationships, other friends. They developed great importance in your eyes, because they became the pathways to being nurtured.

If, then, a new friend doesn't call you for several days, you may realistically fear you have lost a friend. But if nurturing was a problem for you when you were growing up, or if this is your only friend on whom you are depending for nurturing, you may become anxious. If, in addition, you were abandoned as a child, and so are really concerned that you are not likable or will be lonely, your anxiety may become very severe. However, if you have many friends, or know that you can make friends easily, your nurturing needs will not be so threatened, and you will only be sad, not anxious.

Lauren's anxiety had a different origin. Lauren had never failed at anything; she was an "exceptional child." But her self-esteem depended on her being exceptional. Her parents had always approved of and admired her. In fact, they heaped so much praise on her for her successes, that she irrationally felt that their approval of her depended on her continued successes. Each exam, therefore, created severe anxiety; she felt that her parent's esteem as well as her own were riding on the results. She had never learned that she could survive failure. An exam is no longer just an exam if you have bet your life on it.

And some people have nonspecific, "free-floating" anxiety. If you have had some bad experiences that shake your confidence in yourself, that make you doubt your ability to effectively cope with difficult situations, you may have anxiety in any situation you see as dangerous. There may be certain trigger situations you see as dangerous. There may be certain trigger situations that create anxiety for you, or you may feel that the world in general is dangerous and be anxious about a lot of things.

Thus, you may some day be called upon for an answer in class. If you have high self-esteem, are secure in your relationships, and are confident of your ability, then a wrong answer is only one wrong answer. But if right answers are your only pathway to self-esteem, to being liked and nurtured, and to feelings of confidence and security, then a wrong answer isn't just a wrong answer, it can be a major catastrophe for you. If all this is riding on the answer to a question, it is understandable if you panic, and forget everything you ever knew.

Fear is a rather realistic assessment of a situation. It helps you cope. If a bull elephant is charging down on you, fear helps you get out of the way. If you know an exam is coming and you are unprepared, fear helps you study. Fear make you more alert; your mind works better, and more efficiently.

Anxiety is Inefficient

Anxiety, however, is inefficient; it gets in the way of your thinking clearly. As anxiety increases, you find yourself not being able to understand or remember what you are reading. In an exam, a little fear probably makes your mind clear; a little anxiety, and your mind turns off. Then you can't remember things you knew just an hour before, things you remember easily ten minutes after the exam is over.

Instead of helping you run faster, anxiety pours concrete in your shoes. Anxiety makes you yell at the friend who forgot to call you (a behavior not especially helpful to relationships). Anxiety makes you tongue-tied and awkward when you talk to your instructor.

Anxiety is a compelling emotion. It is not something you can ignore. Everyone has some anxieties, but when excessive, they can be terribly destructive.

How Is Anxiety Created?

To demonstrate one way that anxiety is created and how it can affect your life, I am going to teach you math. Let us start by your adding 5678 to 6789 in your head. You have 10 seconds. No one can do this under pressure. Ten seconds later I ring a bell, and say "Well? Everyone is waiting for you." You undoubtedly feel frustrated, humiliated, and angry as you admit failure. Now I say, "Ready for the next lesson?" As you look at others in the class looking at you, you break out in a sweat. You already know you are going to fail. "Multiply 45 by 67." No way;

it can't be done when you are anxious; instead you fantasize how everyone is thinking, "How dumb!" After 10
seconds I ring the bell, and say, "You're not very good at
math, are you? Would you like to learn some more?" You
say, with feeling, "No, thank you!" I have, in less than
a minute, created somebody who will never willingly
open a math book, and for whom the mere mention of
math (or the sight of me) will cause anxiety.

What happened? How did I do this? Everyone has some
fear of failure, which is reasonable. But I just attached
some heavy baggage to that fear. I implied, and you believed, that if you fail, you risk your self-esteem, your
relationships, and your competence. Not true, of course,
but if you buy into that, then you are risking feeling
ashamed, embarrassed, and humiliated. Now, fear of failure has turned to performance anxiety.

Anxious? Who's Anxious?

One way to deal with performance anxiety is to avoid
situations in which you might fail. For example, if you
have math anxiety, you might avoid any book that mentions numbers in the title. As long as you can avoid any
mention, perception, or thought, of math, there is no
anxiety. An interesting question: is there anxiety if it can
be avoided by not seeing a math book? Or is the avoidance
of math evidence of anxiety? Most people who avoid anxiety say, "Oh, no. I just don't have any talent for math (or
art, or music, etc)." Personally, I don't believe them. I
believe that they have *told* themselves they have no talent, that somewhere in the past they had a bad experience
(which they may not even remember), and that they have

simply spent their lives avoiding that particular field and the anxiety that goes with it.

Thus, you can avoid feelings of anxiety by goofing off at the beach. Or you don't even have to go as far as the beach to avoid anxiety. You can just "go away" in your head. You are "studying" but you just can't understand what you are reading. You are "listening" in class and you just can't follow the discussion. If you "go away" for a while, or even go to sleep, you may be giving yourself a message. Maybe it is really boring, and you aren't interested; or maybe, just maybe, you are indulging in anxiety-reducing behavior.

If opening a book produces anxiety (as it sometimes does), and if you can reduce this anxiety by putting the book down, you may be tempted to do so. That doesn't avoid the real consequences of not studying. However it is often easier to avoid anxiety-producing circumstances than it is to cope with the anxiety itself.

There is a story about a visitor to the Big City who, early in the morning, sees the Local Character carry a big drum to the center of the park and start to beat it. At noon he takes a sandwich from his pocket and eats it while he continues to beat the drum; and at sundown he packs up his drum and goes home, only to return the following morning. The visitor, curious, finally asks him, "Why do you beat this drum all day in the park?" Answers the L.C., "Why, to keep away the lions and the tigers, of course." "But there are no lions and tigers in the Big City" argues the visitor. "See," says the L.C., "it works!"

As long as what you are doing "works" and keeps away anxiety, you are likely to keep doing it. Who knows what might happen if you stop? As long as you keep beating your drum, you will not feel anxious.

However, you cannot avoid anxiety-producing situations in college. You have to take some math or science or history; you have to take exams in these subjects, and you have to enter situations that remind you of past humiliations and defeats. There is no way you can avoid such situations, but you can learn to deal with the anxiety they cause.

Coping With Exam Anxiety

The worst source of anxiety in college is taking exams. The week before exam time, the anxiety level in colleges all over the country begins to rise, until the cumulative anxiety, if harnessed, could supply all the energy this country needs to put fifteen shuttles into space.

What can you do about this, personally?

In coping with anxiety, there are three separate areas to consider. These are: 1) coping with the situation causing the anxiety; 2) coping with your own messages of low self-esteem, loss of nurturing, and inadequacy; and 3) coping with the feeling of anxiety itself. Let's look at these three separately, as they relate to taking exams.

Coping with the Situation

Of course, the best way to reduce exam anxiety is to efficiently and effectively prepare for the exam, by spending enough time studying, learning what you have to know. Time can be either your friend or your enemy. You can make time your friend, by leaving enough time to cover the subject adequately. Don't wait until the last week, the last day, the last minute. You know how much work is enough; spread it out over the whole term. If you study enough all term long, you will cope well with the exam without last minute panic.

Very often, as you start a new subject in college, you will have a feeling of confusion. The material may not make sense, or there may be too much of it. But if you put in your time and stay with it, gradually you will gain a feeling of familiarity and "that wasn't as bad as you expected." Some people study the material word by word until they have mastered it; others scan it over and over until it makes sense. Whatever works for you is fine; and when you begin to understand and remember the material, you will achieve a very pleasant feeling of competence and adequacy. Nothing else can give you as wonderful a sense of confidence as mastering a situation that once frightened you to death.

Coping With Your Own Messages

I said that anxiety is a message you send yourself, a false message that in order to feel good about yourself, have good relationships, and feel effective, you must do well on your exam. If you don't do well you are a "failure." Your personal definition of failure may vary from getting an F to not getting an A$^+$. But however we define failure, we fear it because often failure is not just failure, it also means to us that we are worthless, ineffective, and unlovable.

Therefore, when you are experiencing performance anxiety and fear of failure, remind yourself that you really are a very competent person. Your competence is not the issue; passing the exam is the issue. You will remain the same competent person after the exam that you were before.

Also, remind yourself that you are a good person, and your worth as a person is not dependent on your grade. Don't tie your self-esteem to your grades. If you get a good grade, that's nice; but you are not a better person than you were before. You are not testing your worth on this exam; only how much you studied. You will be the same person afterward as before.

Furthermore, if you have friends and family who love you, you will continue to be loved in spite of what happens on this exam. It is not true that your friends and relationships will abandon you if you fail. No one loves you more because you pass or fail an exam.

In other words, separate out the fear, which is natural, from the heavy load of losing your friends, your self-esteem, and your belief in your competence. If you fail you'll still be a good person who is loved and competent.

Make little stickers that say, "I am a good person, I am loved, I am effective." Paste them on the back of your hand, and refer to them frequently before and during the exam. They will help you more than crib notes.

With these things out of the way, you can more easily make the situation into a problem that has a solution. If you were giving someone else advice in this situation, what would you say? Perhaps all you need is reassurance. Perhaps you need help, time, and more experience. All of this is available to you in college.

And you can even use fear as reasonable motivation; if you aren't anxious, but are just afraid you haven't studied enough, you are probably right.

If, in the past, you had a really terrible experience with

exams, math, art, sports, or the opposite sex, so that you felt frustrated, humiliated, and a complete failure, you may not be able to reassure yourself so easily. When you are confronted with a similar situation, you may think, "No way. I won't go through this again."

You have two choices. You can turn tail and run. Many do. You wouldn't be alone.

Or you can back off a little, just far enough for the anxiety to begin to subside. You might do this by saying to yourself, "O.K., I don't have to do anything right now. Let me think about it."

In thinking about your past failures, you can say to yourself, "Maybe I have made a mess of this before. But that doesn't prove I'm hopelessly incompetent. Maybe I was just too young, or I didn't know enough yet, or I didn't get the right kind of help."

When you look at your failures in the light of day, they may not be as bad as you might have thought. Sometimes you can forgive yourself for what was not your fault, or for having been very young. And you can't possibly have gotten where you are now without some failures, and lots of successes. Perhaps you don't value your successes enough. Your "internal critics" may tell you that your triumphs are less important than your defeats. Spend some time shining up your successes. They can look pretty sparkly. And sometimes with a little humor, your early embarrassments can make good stories.

Also, ask yourself, what is the worst that can happen? If more than three terrible things come to mind, sit down and make a list. It can get to be an impressive list. Write down what you are most afraid of. Don't worry about whether these are realistic, rational fears or not. Just write them down.

Look at the list, and ask yourself. If all these terrible things happen, would you live or die? Would you survive? If your first answer is no, think again. Is character built on success or on failure?

But then ask yourself: What is the best that could happen? Imagine the way you would like things to turn out, some wouldn't-it-be-nice-if, happenings. Do a little fantasizing. Remember that prophecies can be self-fulfilling.

Now tell yourself, it probably won't turn out to be the best you could hope for, but it won't be the worst you could fear, either. It will be somewhere in the middle. Imagine what that could be, and get comfortable with it. After all, that's probably how life will be, and what you are going to have to live with. To do this may take courage, stubborness, and the willingness to experience some psychic pain. That will have to come from inside you.

Coping With the Anxiety Itself

Finally, deal with the feeling of anxiety itself, and the effects it has on your body.

As you imagine the terrible consequences of failure, that is, that you will be incompetent, helpless, rejected, abandoned, and worthless, you will have various uncomfortable physiological responses. Where in your body do *you* experience these feelings?

Some people have tightness of the muscles in the neck. If the forehead muscles also contract, they may have a tension headache. Other muscles may tighten and cause pain, in the shoulders, or back. Your heart may beat faster or harder, and drop a beat or two. Your skin may feel drawn and pale if your blood vessels contract; or you may feel hot and sweaty if they dilate. If the blood pools in these dilated vessels, there may be inadequate flow to the brain, so you feel faint and dizzy, and may even pass out. The intestinal muscles may start working harder, so that you develop cramps, or nausea, or loose bowels; or you may just lose your appetite.

Is there anything you can do while you are still conscious? Well, yes, there are a few things. Here are some of them.

1. STOP! Just stop. Stop thinking, stop doing. Sit down in a comfortable chair. When your mind keeps going around and around, things seem to get worse and worse.

2. *Take a deep breath.* Take another. Don't take too many, though, or you may hyperventilate and get lightheaded. Indeed, if you are lightheaded or feel short of breath from over breathing, don't make it worse by continuing to take deep breaths. Just take one or two, then resume normal breathing.

3. *Relax your muscles.* Sitting in a comfortable chair, shut your eyes and relax all your muscles. A good way to do this is to systematically tighten and relax every muscle in your body, group by group. Start at the top of your head and work your way down to your toes. Tighten each group of muscles until you can feel them; then let them go soft. If they are already tight, tighten them more before you relax them. Pay attention to your forehead and neck and shoulders and arms and each finger. Continue down your chest and abdomen and legs and toes.

4. *Give your anxiety a suds number.* In Chapter V I described a SUDS scale. Use that scale to define your feeling of anxiety. Where in your body do you feel it? What SUDS number would you give it? When you feel anxious, you are experiencing a bodily sensation caused by your physical reactions. Giving it a SUDS number gives you a little more control over it, often just enough so that the feeling of anxiety will subside.

5. *Call your anxiety anticipation.* The meaning you give to that sensation is actually up to you; it is under your control. You can just as easily interpret it as a sensation of anticipation. Every actor appearing on the stage experiences it! It helps the actor perform better! Allow it to help you.

6. *Talk about it.* Talk about your concerns; ventilate them. Spread them out in the light and get a good look at them. Find someone who will listen to you. Preferably this will be someone with the wonderful qualifications of being able to listen without giving advice, and without telling you that you shouldn't feel that way. (If you know such a person, treasure him or her; such people are hard to find.)

7. *Explore your feelings.* What exactly are you feeling besides anxiety? Sometimes anxiety keeps you from your real feelings. Define your feelings as clearly as you can. It makes them much easier to look at. Sometimes feelings are difficult to define; for example, anxiety and anticipation may feel almost the same. Don't defend or justify your thoughts and feelings. They just are. It is even better if you can *express* those feelings; if you feel like crying, do so. You will feel better afterwards (unless you tie yourself up in knots by thinking you shouldn't feel that way, or you shouldn't cry.)

8. *Draw your feelings.* Sometimes feelings are hard to put into words. Using colors, *draw* the way you feel. Keep a drawing journal and pastels handy for such purposes. You can often create a picture that is far more expressive than words.

9. *Go for a run.* Run around the block. Exercise, especially on a regular basis, is excellent for reducing anxiety. In some way not yet fully understood, exercise is a physiological anxiety reducer, that enhances the natural anti-anxiety chemicals in the brain and body (the endorphins). Sometimes it induces a meditative state; sometimes even a "natural high."

10. *Anchor some good feelings.* Reap the benefits of Exercise 7 (anchoring good feelings.) This is the time to use those feelings. Squeeze your left arm with your right hand, and recall all those good feelings you had anchored for use at a time like this.

11. *Be good to yourself.* Do something good for yourself that makes you feel cared for, even if you have to care for yourself. Give yourself a treat. Don't take addictive substances; they work too well. But how about a sybaritic hot bath with lots of suds? Hot tubs are very big in California. If you are not addicted to food and it's a real emergency, you might buy yourself a (small) ice cream sundae with hot fudge, whipped cream, nuts, and a cherry.

12. *Meditate.* Meditation has many uses: for physical relaxation and reducing tension, for clearing the mind, for promoting the flow of ideas, for improving serenity, for turning off left brain chatter and reducing external stimulation, and for inducing altered states of consciousness. When you are anxious or under stress, it is a place to which you can always withdraw for a moment to get centered. When confronted by problems, it is a place where you can always get in touch with your own inner wisdom.

There are many meditation techniques; learn one. There are many different ways to meditate; I do not think one way is better than another. Read Herbert Benson's *The Relaxation Response,* or Robert Ornstein's *The Psychology of Consciousness.*

When I am beginning to feel fragmented, I find the following "centering meditation" useful.

First, get comfortable. Then look around the room and silently identify various objects by name. Notice that though you have been in the place you are in for some time, you had lost awareness of these objects. Looking at them and naming them brings them back to the foreground of your consciousness. But now look at them in a different way, as though you were an abstract painter, noticing only patterns, light, shadows, and colors.

Close your eyes. (Of course, you can't read this with your eyes shut. Either you will have to have somebody read it aloud to you, or you can tape it slowly and play it back, or you can just remember what it says.)

Now, listen for and identify any sounds you hear. Then just listen to them as though you were a modern composer, as though they were sounds made by the instruments of an orchestra.

Now, with your eyes still shut, identify anything that your skin is touching. What is it in your skin that allows you to make that identification? How do you do that? What are the sensations?

What is the position of your body, and of your arms and legs? How do you know? What is the sensation?

Examine the sensation in your muscles that tells you whether they are relaxed or tense. Don't change them; just note them. In the same way, examine your breathing, as you breathe in and out. Note the rhythm, the change in temperature in your throat, the movement of your chest and of your diaphragm, the feeling in your abdominal muscles. Note any other sensations in your abdomen or in your pelvis.

Somewhere in your body, you are apt to feel a place you identify as more truly *you* than anywhere else. If you feel such a place, concentrate on it for a few moments as if it were your center.

Now slowly, gently, come back, open your eyes, and look around. If you are with other people who have been doing what you have been doing, look at someone and see how he looks. Make contact with him with your eyes. Then break contact and go back to your center. Open your eyes and make contact again, and break it and go back to your center.

Now Let's Get Down to Work

So you see, there are many things you can do to reduce anxiety. You don't have to do them all at the same time. Try them all out. See what works best for you. Once you have learned how to cope well with anxiety in college, you will have learned a great deal about coping with life.

But finally, you have to act. Anxiety can be immobilizing and self-perpetuating. Sometimes, you have to pick yourself up and face your feared consequences. You often have to function in spite of anxiety. So get to work, take the exam, and get on with your life. Remember, these may be the best years of your life. Enjoy them!

Accept Your Body's Reactions

A word about those physical reactions to anxiety which, although harmless, can cause frightening sensations. Even if you know these symptoms can be caused by anxiety, you may not be *sure*. Perhaps you think, "Maybe I really have heart trouble, or cancer or some other dread disease." Anxiety breeds anxiety. When you are anxious, these sensations can be frightening, so that you become more anxious, and develop even more symptoms. It is then easy to convince yourself that there is something wrong with you; you need "calcium" or "supervitamins" or have contracted a fatal disease.

When you feel this way, the logical, rational thing to do is to go down to the health center to check it out. It may not be that easy, however, because when you are gripped by anxiety, you can also lose your confidence and doubt your worth. You may imagine the medical staff will laugh at you, telling you it is all in your head, and that you need a shrink. Anxiety begets its own anxieties.

I think it is important to check out these fears about your health, and not just live with them. There are no rewards for ignoring symptoms, even those due to anxiety. It doesn't make you a better person. At least half of what your health center does is reassure students; it is an important part of their job. They *won't* laugh at you for checking yourself out; probably they will tell you it was a good thing to do.

Unable to deal with her anxiety in college, Lauren dropped out and, immobilized by anxiety, experienced real failure. For a year, she lived in a small, scruffy room and watched television soaps. But when her parents and friends stayed by her and she didn't perish, she finally accepted that her life did not depend on "success." She returned to college and, having learned to cope with her performance anxiety, went on to a brilliant career.

11 Anger

We were sitting in the school lounge. "What," I asked, "do you get angry about in college?" The students looked at me to see if I was serious, and then started reeling off grievances.

"Academic pressures."

"The amount of homework."

"Teachers' unrealistic expectations."

"Deadlines."

"People!"

"The world!"

"Sororities," said Mary, an attractive young woman, Sororities are the worst." The others nodded. "Really? Sororities? I would never have guessed that. Why sororities?"

"I cried more about sororities than about anything else."

"Why? What's that all about?"

"Well, take rushing. You put on a nice little dress, and visit the sorority house. They seat you on a couch, and there's some lemonade and cookies, and they sit on the floor, and start asking you questions about how much money your father makes, and where you go on vacations, and what kind of car you have, and then they write letters to people in your hometown to check up on you." Others chimed in. "And they're telling you to just be natural, while you're trying to say what you think they want to hear." "Then they tell you how much they really love you, the first week, without even knowing you." Mary agreed. "When I feel bad, I always go talk with a friend who isn't in the house. You're afraid to tell anyone in the house how you really feel." A young man said, "It's the same with fraternities. The Greeks are really intimidating. If you don't belong to a house, you're *nothing!*" An attractive young woman nodded. "Last year, a boy I met asked me which house I was in, and when I said I didn't belong to a sorority, he just turned around and walked away. I was so mad!"

"What is your name?" I asked.

"Jennie."

"Jennie, I'm really interested. What did you do when you got so mad?"

"What *could* I do? I felt like bashing his head in, but I just went for a run. When I get mad, I just go for a run until I feel better."

"What did you think of him?"

"He's an inconsiderate, spoiled, self-centered bastard. I'd like to kill him!"

"He really did it to you, didn't he? It's like he knew just where to place the stiletto . . ."

Jennie began to cry. "I was so lonely then, and I wanted so much to be liked . . ."

Anger has many dimensions. It may be felt as only a minor annoyance, directed at a minor nuisance. It may increase to irritation, and escalate to resentment. We can experience righteous anger, and overpowering rage. We can conceal, suppress, ignore, or otherwise "bag" our anger, perhaps without even being aware of it, until one day our bag explodes, and we disappear in a cloud of smoke and steam. We can harness our anger and, like a steam locomotive, get a lot of mileage out it. Or we may pop off frequently like a string of firecrackers, creating "sound and fury, signifying nothing."

Anger is an emotion that is difficult to deal with, in ourselves and in others. Whether minimal or extreme, it is an important emotion, too important to ignore, and too important to let control you. Let's try to put a handle on it.

Physically, anger causes a series of temporary changes in the body, much like those of fear, but oriented more toward fight than flight. We begin to pump out adrenalin and noradrenalin, so our skin either flushes or becomes pale, depending on which hormone is in greater concentration. Both hormones make our hearts beat faster and stronger, making more blood available to our bodies. Our blood pressure increases, our muscles tense for action, our reflexes become faster, we become stronger, we feel less pain. We are ready to *attack*.

Anger Occurs
When We Are Frustrated

Anger is one of the four basic human emotions (glad, sad, mad, scared.) We feel anger when one of our pathway goals is frustrated. You remember that our basic needs (caring, self-esteem, etc.) are filled by achieving goals, which in turn are reached through one of several pathways. The strength of the anger depends on how much our basic need depends on the particular pathway goal being frustrated.

Jenny's basic needs in this particular instance were self-esteem and caring relationships. The extent to which this obnoxious young man frustrated those needs was directly related to the degree of her anger. If Jenny already had good self-esteem and relationships, she would have been much less angry than if she identified this young man as the major pathway to these goals.

We all want to be treated with respect. If we are treated with disrespect and become angry, it is because we need that respect for our own self-respect. If we experience rudeness, we become angry to the extent to which it threatens our need to be liked.

What Do We Do With This Anger?

1. *Blaming.* When we are angry, we almost always immediately blame the person who made us angry, who frustrated our pathway goal. He is a terrible person. Get the bastard! Righteous anger really feels good.

2. *Dumping.* Some always express their anger immediately and directly. That isn't necessarily bad; many people get it out right away, and feel fine afterward. It becomes a problem when they "dump" on others, giving guilt shots, righteously blaming others for their feelings, and verbally blowing them away. Physically, they can "act it out," and attack. They have no mechanism for dealing with anger other than by hurting someone, verbally or physically. They are said to "have a temper," and people treat them with circumspection.

3. *Bagging anger.* Many of us "bag" our angers. We don't really know what to do with it, so we try not to let it show, and even try not to feel it. Some of us have been doing that since childhood. Alice Miller thinks a lot of us have been doing that.* Each such incident is added to others, building up resentment and hostility day by day, until a final straw makes the whole bag explode.

4. *Kick the dog.* Sometimes we "kick a dog"; that is, we displace our anger onto innocent people. When we are carrying a load of anger about something, your roommate who comes in the door and says "Hello" can get it, *pow*, right in the kisser, and says in amazement, "What did I do?"

5. *Passive-aggressiveness.* Sometimes we become "passive-aggressive." That is, when we have trouble expressing anger, we can express it indirectly by procrastinating, dragging our heels, and forgetting to do things. (When your roommate "forgets" and leaves her wet towel on

---

* *Thou Shalt Not Be Aware* (New York: New American Library, 1986).

your bed for the fifth time, ask, "Are you upset about something?")

6. *Repression.* Others, attempting to control their anger, push it down so far it goes completely out of sight and out of mind—and into the body. Physically, this often leaves them tense, with tight muscles, or chronic high blood pressure, for "no good reason." And the anger always comes out somewhere else, often unexpectedly.

7. *Anger turned inward.* Sometimes we turn the anger inward, against ourselves. We blame ourselves, believe we are "bad," and prove it by, for example, punishing ourselves harshly, or getting into trouble over and over.

8. *Depression.* If we feel futile, worthless, helpless, and hopeless, our anger can turn into depression.

9. *Addictions.* And sometimes people use chemicals or food to avoid feeling angry, and become addicted.

Some Erroneous Concepts About Anger

Much of this occurs because we have developed some concepts about anger that may not be true. Let's look at some of these ideas.

For example, you may believe you are helpless in the grip of your feelings, and have no options but to act on them. If, instead of going for a run, Jennie had been "overcome by rage," she could have picked up a rock and killed the young man, believing that she "couldn't help herself." This belief in your helplessness is nonsense. People are not in control of what they feel, but they are certainly in charge of what they do about it. Their belief that they

are not in charge is a self-fulfilling prophecy, and dangerous.

Another notion is that if you talk about your angry
feelings, you are more likely to act on them. In fact, the
opposite is true. Jennie might have been so embarrassed
by her anger, or so afraid of what we would think of her,
that she might not have told us about it. But having told
us about it, she felt much better. Ventilation helps clear
out angry feelings. In order to deal with our feelings and
control them, we must be able to identify, acknowledge,
and confront them. If we deny them, our feelings will
eventually control us.

You may have been taught that anger is wrong and that
you are "bad" for having anger. Actually, anger is not the
best emotion of which people are capable; but it is not
"bad" or "evil," and *you* are not "bad" or "evil," but
human. For better or worse, it goes with our territory, it
is part of our genetic inheritance. We all need to learn
how to deal with it.

You may believe that your anger is O.K. if you can
justify it by blaming the person who made you angry.
Then the other person is "bad," and you are "righteous."
(Everyone in the student lounge took a turn saying how
awful the young man who turned away from Jennie was.)
This theme of righteous anger has been a destructive
thread throughout all human history.

Another faulty assumption is that we are and should
always be rational. We sometimes like to think that we
behave the way we do because we think logically. Then
along comes anger, and we demonstrate, over and over
again, that our behavior is not based on reason alone. In
fact, all emotions are nonrational. If our nonrational be-

havior makes us uncomfortable, we make up a story about why we are angry so that we *seem* to be rational; we "rationalize" our behavior so that we will be less uncomfortable.

Our Anger Can Make Us Anxious

Our own anger can make us anxious.

An angry person who does not know how to handle anger may be destructive and dangerous, to himself and others. We may experience anxiety about anger for good reason. We may be afraid we will hurt others.

More often, however, people have a belief in the power of the anger itself to hurt others and cause bad things to happen. This is "magical thinking," as in Stephen King's book *Firestarter*, in which a little girl who gets angry at others makes them catch on fire.

Also, we may be anxious that if we show anger, it may offend people whom we love or need, and they will leave us.

When we are able to deal with anger well and learn to use it constructively, then it need not be either destructive or anxiety-producing.

Although anger itself is a perfectly normal emotion, too much or unbridled anger is not. Therefore, if you have been bagging resentment until it blows up, or have angry explosions that are disturbing you or others, or are just feeling anxious about your anger, it may be a good idea to talk to a counselor.

However, even if your anger is minimal and easily controlled, it will help if you understand it better.

Later we will consider how to deal with the anger of others. But first let us deal with your own anger.

Coping With Your Own Anger

In dealing with your own anger, whether minimal or severe, I suggest the following steps.

1. First, allow the anger to exist without denying it. Before you do anything else, *notice* that you are angry. Say (to yourself) "I am angry," or as Jennie said, "I was so mad." Introduce a crucial pause; a recognition of what is happening, so that you do not immediately and reflexively act on your anger. That recognition, and that pause, are *crucial* in learning to deal with anger. "Count to ten."

2. Find some way of expressing this anger, privately and safely. Do not dump it violently and aggressively on other people. Find some physical way of acting it out in a harmless manner. Anger causes many important physiological changes in you that are directed toward *action*.

Inhibiting action causes damage to the body: muscle spasm, headaches, high blood pressure. But the action need not be directed at the cause of the anger, pleasurable as that might feel. Jennie said, "When I get mad, I go for a run." Excellent. One woman I know buys cheap china to throw against a fence in her yard. "Batakas," firm pillows with handles, are sold for the express purpose of hitting beds or floors to release your rage. Jump up and down; chop some wood; join a football team, go for a run, play squash.

Being cut off by someone while driving is a dangerous situation for many, including me, because there is no good, safe way to physically express the anger, and I have a dangerous weapon in my hands. I try shouting, and tell myself that trading dangerous acts with a nut would make me as crazy as the nut.

In addition to expressing your anger physically (but harmlessly), express it verbally, to a third party. Mary said she talks to a friend, who is not in her sorority. Everyone needs such a person, who will listen while you blow off steam. Really get into it, and let it all out. It doesn't hurt anyone, and it feels good, especially if the listening person doesn't try to be too helpful or give advice. Other times, make sure that you listen to your friend's anger. Everyone needs a listener now and then. Just nod your head and say things like, "Isn't it awful?"

Expressing your anger is good for you. It's good to blow off steam so that you don't blow up or get high blood pressure. By itself, however, just expressing anger in this way does very little for you. Many people treat life as a series of little explosions, and never learn any better way of dealing with frustration. After you have let the steam out, don't stop there; *do* something about it.

3. After your physical exertion, wait for your physiological reactions to subside. Don't do anything until your blood pressure and your heart rate return to normal. This may seem like a long five to ten minutes. Establish an inflexible rule for yourself; do nothing until your pulse and blood pressure are normal. In order to let these reactions subside as quickly as possible after your physical exertion, practice complete muscle relaxation for a few minutes. Sit quietly, shut your eyes, take a few deep breaths, and then relax your muscles, one at a time, until you are back to normal. How you feel affects how you think, so try to be honest with yourself. In the grip of anger, you may think you are seeing things rationally, but believe me, you are not.

4. Then, get in touch with the need that is being frustrated. You can do this by asking yourself, what is it you would have liked? What is it you wanted and didn't get? What would you like to happen?

Anger always means that some important want or need is being frustrated or threatened. What Mary and the others were talking about was their need for self-respect, which was frustrated and threatened by the way in which the sorority people were treating them. Jennie's encounter with the young Greek was the ultimate in disrespect for her as a person. When you are angry, it is important to take the anger back to this unmet need or want. This may be hard to do when all you want to do is to punch someone out. Do it anyway. It is an important step in learning to deal with anger.

5. When you are in touch with that need for self-respect (or security, caring, or whatever), affirm yourself. Say to yourself, "I am really *entitled* to respect (or security, or caring)." The main problem is, that you begin to doubt yourself. When Jennie's young man walked away, part of her anger was related to his shaking her confidence in herself and her worth. No one is so secure that someone cannot introduce some doubt. It is important to confront this, and to reassure yourself.

One way of reassuring yourself is to imagine how you would feel if you had gotten what you wanted. If Jennie's young man had said, "How wonderful," how would that have made her feel? If she could remember that feeling, then her feelings of self-worth and confidence would have come back.

6. Finally, remember that you have more than one way

of filling your needs. You have a whole quiver full of arrows. You always have access to alternative ways of getting what you need for yourself. When you are angry, you may forget this, and think there is only one way to get what you need.

I suspect Jennie had a thought that, consciously or unconsciously, went something like this: "It is so difficult to fill my need (for self-esteem, love, security) . . . someone has made me suspect I may never be happy . . . he is a terrible person . . . I would like to kill him."

He may be indeed be a terrible person. I don't know him. More important is that he succeeded in making Jennie insecure and anxious about herself.

Almost always there is an underlying fear that your needs will never be met. On some level, you doubt your value. You suddenly feel ugly, unlovable and worthless. Your fate is in the hands of another person, who has let you down. You have put your eggs in the wrong basket, and they are broken. You will never feel good about yourself again.

You may have an awful feeling of "impasse," that there is *no way* to get your need met. This is not just a temporary setback, this is the end of the world. Confront that feeling of "impasse." Jennie has to begin to think, "Really, now, I do have other sources of self-esteem. My life doesn't depend on this young man whom I don't even know. I don't even want to know people like him anyway. People who know me like me, and I *will* have a good time in college."

When you feel in an impasse, start exploring other ways of meeting your needs. People are remarkably resourceful and inventive. When you are anxious about anger and your SUDS rise, your mind may turn off for a while, and you may not be able to *think* of other ways to meet your needs. However, there are *always* other ways, perhaps not as easy, direct or immediately satisfying, but then life is like that. Sometimes the alternate way turns out to be better than the original way.

Always have a second and even a third back-up plan ready for things that are important for you. Keep a second and third arrow in your quiver. Keep making contingency plans. Remember Murphy's law: "Anything that can go wrong will, and at the worst possible moment." Just knowing in advance that things don't always work at first, helps you meet adversity when it comes.

"Keep Your Damned Jack!"

Sometimes anger stems from the belief that you should get what you want or need, perhaps without even asking for it. You may believe that if you have to ask, it isn't worth getting. Or you may be reluctant to ask, because you might be turned down.

Do you know the "keep your damned jack" story?

A man driving on a lonely country road gets a flat, and finds he doesn't have a jack with which to change the tire. He remembers a farmhouse about five miles back, and starts to walk toward it, thinking the people there will undoubtedly lend him a jack, offer him a drink, even give him a ride back. As he walks, he thinks, maybe not the drink or the ride, but at least, they'll lend him the jack. Then he thinks, maybe he'll arrive at dinnertime, and they won't want to be bothered. Maybe even they are cantankerous people who don't like strangers. Maybe

they are nasty, no-good so-and-so's who wouldn't do anyone a favor even if he was dying!

At this point he arrives at the house and knocks on the
door. A man answers and says, "Yes?" to which our hero
replies, "Keep your damned jack!" and hits him in the
face.

Don't forget to at least ask, before you get angry and hit
someone in the face. You might be pleasantly surprised.
People who ask pleasantly and assertively for what they
want get it about half the time. People who don't ask,
don't get.

Communicating Anger

The question arises, if you are angry at someone, should
you let that person know? I think in general, you should,
but nonviolently, and without laying a guilt trip. Be aware
that your anger is powerful. Never, ever, blow the other
person away; that serves no useful purpose at all. If you
have tried several ways to get something, and you have
concluded that you aren't going to get it, and if you believe that your relationship with the other person is suffering because of it, then expressing your anger judiciously
is an excellent attention-getting device. It lets the other
person know that you are taking your frustration seriously, it is important to you. If you do it right, it also lets
the other person know that he or she is important to you.
But be aware that the other person is going to have reactions to your anger of defensiveness, fear, or anger in
return.

We often have trouble expressing anger to people we
love. Our ability to love and to be angry with the same
person at the same time creates a conflict within us. Peo-

ple are apt to believe that good and bad feelings cannot co-exist, and that if you are angry, you cannot also be loving. It is important to make it clear that that you can love people at whom you feel angry, and that being angry does not mean you are rejecting the person. Let the other person know he or she is important to you (e.g., "I'm saying this because you're valuable to me, and I don't want our relationship to end because of this." Or, "I want you to know that just because I'm mad at you doesn't mean I don't like you").

And don't come on blaming or correcting, like a critical parent. You can avoid this by accepting at least some responsibility for your anger, by saying it is your need that is not being filled. Otherwise the element of blame inherent in anger is difficult for people to accept. Some need of yours is involved; otherwise you wouldn't be angry. That doesn't mean it isn't a legitimate need, or that you shouldn't be angry. But it helps a lot to be aware of your own need, and it helps the other person for you to say it out loud.

If the interchange is with a stranger, or with someone who is not important to you, the same rules should apply. Assume that everyone in this world is of value, and you will get along much better with everyone.

It's O.K. To Get Help

Sometimes it may seem that anger just can't be handled. The most common cause of anger that you can't handle is an underlying feeling that people are uncaring, stupid, bad, and, most important, not taking good enough care of you. This is often due to a feeling of a bottomless pit inside, a need for caring that has not yet been filled, and that you still expect others to fill. When they won't, you may be confused and frustrated and blame the other person.

If hearing someone say "No" to what seems a reasonable request always makes you blow up, perhaps you have such a bottomless pit. You may think that if only you got this, or someone did that, you would feel better. If you are disappointed a lot, the problem is more likely to be with that unfilled need than with others. If you walk around mad at the school, your classmates, or the world, then perhaps you have such an unfillable hole. Trying to get others to fill an unfillable hole is an exercise in futility. If this might be true for you, give counseling a try; sometimes it makes the world a better place in which to be.

Coping With Others' Anger

Now that you can cope with your own anger, you should have some insight into coping with the anger of others. Now you know that people who are angry at you are blaming you for something that threatens or frustrates them. It never is only what you have done that angers them. Their anger reflects, instead, their fear and anxiety about *meeting a basic need.* Although directed at you, their anger gives you a quick and revealing look at their inner insecurities and frustrations. It tells you much more about them, than about what you did wrong.

But this is hard to remember when someone is yelling at you. Coping with others' anger has less to do with managing their anger than with managing your own fear and guilt.

The Usual Responses to Anger

Anger directed at you has to create a difficult emotional reaction within you. You may have uncomfortable physiological reactions. That's normal. Don't feel you have to do anything because of these reactions. Some people cry easily when attacked; don't worry about it, or think it a sign of weakness. Just go ahead and do what you have to do anyway. Tears don't have to get in your way. Besides, they evaporate.

The usual, instinctive responses to anger are to either *run, attack, submit,* or *defend.* These are all understandable, but often inappropriate and hardly ever useful.

Don't Run Away

Anger causes fear. That's normal. And fear lends wings to our feet. But nevertheless, in general, don't run away. I say, in general, because sometimes it is the only wise thing to do. Don't tangle with nuts. If some idiot is coming at you with a raised tire iron, make your excuses, lock your door, step on the gas, and absent yourself rapidly. Discretion is often the better part of valor. When, however, the individual is someone with whom you have a relationship, running makes the next encounter more difficult.

Don't Attack Back

Don't attack back. It is natural to want to. Don't do it. You may feel outraged by the attack, and become angry yourself. That is a perfectly normal response. And the fear you feel may also make you angry. By now, however, you should be able to deal with this. Reassure yourself that you are not really at risk, nor is your self-esteem, and other people won't look down on you for not responding with anger. Attacking back might feel good at the moment, but it just escalates the situation, and makes it more difficult to resolve later.

Don't Submit

Don't submit. Anger is often used aggressively to establish dominance and get control. As a way of establishing dominance it has great significance in the animal, academic, and corporate worlds. It establishes a pecking order, as to who is allowed to get angry at whom. Parents get angry at their children, but not vice versa ("Don't you dare use that tone of voice to me, young man (or young lady)!" or, "What right have you to be angry?"). Coaches scream at players. Teachers get sarcastic with students. Going along with it establishes you as a group player; you will get along well in the system, and when your time comes, you can yell at your children and put down your students and those "under" you.

Or you don't have to play that game. Not going along with it will certainly surprise and possibly outrage those who have always played by those rules.

Also, anger is used by some as a way of getting needs met. It is especially common with the "bottomless pit" people. The bigger the hole, the bigger and more frequent the anger. The less you can do to fill it, the more the other person thinks you should do. The anger at not getting basic needs filled is dumped on you. You have become the person responsible for filling that need.

You can decline that honor if you wish. You can choose

to fill needs for others if you wish; but you don't have to. Be aware of the trap in filling such needs: initially doing something for another person may make you feel good, but you may find it hard to stop. If you fill a demanding person's needs, you may become the "official" filler of that need in the future. And if you have been coerced by the other's anger, you have rewarded bullying behavior, and increased the likelihood of being coerced in the future. Beware!

Don't Dexify

Finally, inhibit your natural impulse to DEfend, EXplain, and justIFY. (Remember the acronym DEXIFY.) DON'T DEXIFY to an angry person. It won't work, and you'll just end up feeling foolish. Resist the rather natural impulse to explain why you did what you did, hoping perhaps that the other person will then say, "Oh, I understand; yes, I won't be angry any more." It will never happen! Anger has little to do with *why* you did what you did; only the effect of what you did on the angry person. Asking an angry person to see things from your perspective is almost always asking too much. Your intentions are rarely the issue. While you are defending, justifying, and explaining, the other person often hears you saying, in effect, "You shouldn't feel the way you do." Logic and reason can't be heard very well by someone in the nonrational grip of anger. The greater the anger, the less logic and reason have to do with it.

Be clear about the difference between "dexifying" and apologizing. You don't have to deny making mistakes, and it is all right to apologize for your mistakes; it's rather nice, in fact, and makes other people feel better. You don't have to be abjectly apologetic for living. It is *not* all right to *have* to apologize to avoid someone's wrath, or because you think you are a terrible person for having made mistakes. It's always all right to say, "I blew it. I didn't know. I'm sorry." But don't believe that you shouldn't make mistakes, or that it makes you an awful or inadequate person. Good people make bad mistakes all the time.

Some people seem to believe that mistakes should never be made, that they are the result of stupidity or bad character. Actually mistakes are only the results of decisions made on the best information available to you at the time. Mistakes are never made deliberately. All behavior and experience is the result of taking action, seeing what happens, and modifying future action. If you always know in advance what is going to happen, you live on a planet that is different from mine. Wisdom comes from experience, and experience means making your mistakes and learning from them. Just don't make the same mistake three times.

So, How *Do* You Cope With Angry People?

To cope with angry people, try the following 6 steps.

1. *Stand your ground.* Stand up if the other person is standing over you. Maintain eye contact. Don't accept a one down position physically or symbolically.

Collect your thoughts. Get centered. Accept whatever emotional or physiological responses you have as perfectly normal. You don't have to act on them. Don't react immediately. Listen for the content.

Accept the other's anger as a normal expression of feelings. Convey an attitude of acceptance and understanding. Don't do or say anything that might imply that anger is improper. Like any feeling, it may be irrational, but it is not wrong to have.

2. *"What are you angry about?"* Then ask, "What are you angry about? What did I do?" *(Not,* what did I do *wrong.)* Listen carefully.

Almost always the angry person will blame you for making him angry. You will hear accusations about your intelligence, your morals, your lack of responsibility, your lack of caring. Try not to swallow this hook. People who are angry because they feel deprived or frustrated must generally try to justify it by blaming *you;* it just goes with the territory. Afterward they will probably be embarrassed by what they said. Don't get hooked by these accusations. If you can, let them slide right by. If they bother you, don't react to them for now.

Instead, concentrate on the facts. Find out what the angry person is really angry about. Don't assume you know. Which one of your behaviors triggered this display? What exactly is it that the other person is saying you did? You may be confused about what is actually bothering the other person; ask for clarification. I am sure it will be forthcoming in great detail.

3. *Validate the other's point of view.* Then validate the other person's view of what it is you did. Say, "Yes, I can see that," or, "I can hear how that must have sounded." You don't have to agree that it was wrong, shameful, dishonest, stupid, or any of the dozen or so other allegations that an angry person will make. You can accept the act itself. Don't even think about answering attacks on your motives, morals, or intelligence; sidestep them completely.

4. *"What would you have liked?"* Ask "What should

I have done," "What can I do," or "What would you like me to do?" What you are trying to do is move the person from the terrible sense of unmet basic needs (frustration, loss, low self-esteem, or whatever the feeling is that produced the anger), to what it would take to produce good feelings.

5. *Move the other person to good feelings.* If you are successful, you will notice an immediate change in the quality of the anger; the sense of desperation will be replaced by something else, perhaps a sense of wistful sadness. When that happens you will also notice a feeling of relief in yourself; you can begin to relax, the storm is about to pass. Change your tone of voice to one that is supportive and sympathetic, as you follow-up by asking, "Would that have made things better?" or saying, "Yes, I can see that would have been good." You are now moving in the direction of how the other person would feel if the denied need had been met. That feeling, of needs being met, even in fantasy, cannot co-exist with the feeling of anger about needs not being met.

6. *Now start helping.* Now you can join forces as you seek a cure for the problem. Start being a helper, rather than an obstruction. Now that you understand the terrible predicament of the angry person, in which you were both the means for filling his or her needs, and the obstacle, you can start problem solving together. "What are *we* to do? What can *we* do about this situation?"

All this requires, of course, that you are not "hooked" into any of the four instinctual responses, to run, attack, submit, or defend. It also requires a fair amount of patience, because anger takes a while to subside. The rewards, however, are considerable. You will have learned that anger does not necessarily mean the end of the world

or that relationships are irreparably damaged. The opposite is frequently true. You may become closer. You have
shown the other person that you can understand; that you
are not blown away; and that you can be helpful. You
have discovered that you don't have to fear anger in others.

When you can handle others' anger successfully, you
can choose whether or not you wish to. But don't fool
yourself by saying that you don't *wish* to handle angry
feelings, when you *can't*. You are not really exercising
choice when you have to run, attack, submit, or defend.

Sometimes you may do something, knowing in advance
it might make someone angry. People make choices like
that all the time. You will have to decide for yourself how
important it is to avoid others' anger. You are more likely
to make better choices if you can handle others' anger
well.

When you are not hooked by feelings of shame, fear,
embarrassment, or inadequacy, you will be able to respond to anger empathically, helpfully, and nondefen-
sively.

Meanwhile, back to Jennie. As we finished our discussion in the lounge, she said, "You know, that guy probably will always think that his self-esteem depends on
doing what everyone in his house thinks is right." Mary
added, "Since I joined a house, my G.P.A. went from 3.2
to 2.2, just because I thought I needed their good opinion." Jack chimed in, "I don't pay too much attention to
that. I'm in engineering, and I have to study hard, so I
ignore a lot of what goes on. But I enjoy being in a house."
Jennie concluded, "That's O.K. But it took me a long time
to know that I was all right, even if I didn't join a house.

I guess I'm still not sure, or I wouldn't have gotten so mad at him."

"How do you feel about him now?"

"Now?" she replied. "I sort of feel sorry for him. I don't feel angry at him anymore. But I'm still angry at the system. I may do something about that."

She may, too. Harnessed anger is a powerful tool.

12 Depression

"College Help Line. Can I help you?"
Silence.
"Hello? Hello? Are you there?"
"Uh, I'm sorry. This was a mistake . . ."
"Wait a minute, don't hang up. Talk to me. Maybe we can help."
"No, I don't think so. It's all right."
"Wait a minute. What happened? Tell me."

"Nothing's happened. It's just everything . . . I don't think
I want to talk about it."
"You sound really down. I'd really like to hear about it."
"There's nothing to tell. I'm just feeling really bad."
"I see. Things are going really bad for you."
"I don't think there's any way out."
"You feel really closed in."
Starting to cry, "I don't know what to do."
"Would you like to tell me about it?"

This conversation, or one like it, is going on, right now,
at your college and at many others, all across the country.
Help line phones have been set up to help stem the tide
of hopelessness and helplessness that periodically engulfs
students and others. They are a far better answer than the
barricades one Eastern college puts up over "The Gorge"
at exam time to keep students from jumping.

Information and Misinformation

When we're not depressed, we don't like to think about
depression. When we *are* depressed, we don't want to talk
about it. It's not a high priority topic of conversation, and
misinformation is common. Although there is a lot of
depression in college, you might not be aware of it because
students "cover up." It is often a surprise when a student
commits suicide. There is often administrative denial as
well, denial that gets in the way of good, active programs
that might help students. This is a pity, because there is
much that could be done to help.

Depression can be either short-term or long-term.
Short-term refers to a "crisis", that is, something that had
a clear beginning and, with help, will have a good end

within six weeks. If you are in a short-term depression, you are "reacting" to a particularly bad situation in your life, and when the situation comes under control, you will feel better. Short-term troubles generally respond to crisis therapy. Counseling offices and help lines give emotional support and advice oriented toward such short-term, crisis therapy.

It is common to think, "Nobody can help me." That is never true, and in short-term depression, help is easier to get than you think. What seems overwhelming and insoluble can often be turned around by a fresh viewpoint and a few resources you might not know you have.

Long-term depression has less to do with what is happening right now, and more to do with your family and your biochemistry. Long-term depression generally indicates a need for a more complete workup. College counseling centers will refer you to a trained therapist if it looks as if you need more than counseling.

Much long-term depression is due to a chemical deficiency in your body. This chemical can be replaced with "antidepressants" that will relieve the depression. Don't try to find them in your health food store. You need to see a physician in order to obtain them.

There is also a strong relationship between alcohol and drug addiction, and depression. Recent research shows that much drug or alcohol use is an attempt to self-medicate, to try to find a chemical that will replaces the normal body chemistry. Don't use your body like a test tube when you haven't taken chemistry yet. Go to the experts for advice. Get competent medical help.

Everyone gets a little depressed at times. That is normal, and it is normal to feel good again and begin enjoying life in another day or two. If the depression is more than just a little, and if it is going on for more than a week, if you are depressed to the point where you are not able to study and your grades are suffering, if you have trouble sleeping or eating, if you have been resorting to drugs or alcohol in order to feel better, or if you have been playing with the idea of suicide, then don't fool around. Don't wait for something to happen, or somebody to rescue you. Call your counseling office, or your local hotline, and do it now!

The college suicide rate is alarming. In the last 25 years, in the United States, the suicide rate among young college men and women has gone up approximately 250 percent. Young people ages 15 to 24 now constitute almost one-fifth of the more than 27,000 known suicides in the country each year.*

There are, of course, many routes to suicide, but if I were to try to produce a suicidal depression in you, I would start before college, by having you believe that you are not valued by your family, or are valued for the wrong reasons; I would have you seriously doubt your value to anyone. I would make you responsible for the well-being of at least one mixed-up parent, whom you would, from time to time, disappoint, and whose loss, paradoxically, would fill you with futility and hopelessness. I would make sure you felt that no one can understand your situation, and that there is no point in trying to explain how you feel to others. Then, when things go wrong (as they do for everyone now and then), I would suggest that you blame yourself, see it as more evidence of your own incompetence and lack of worth, and isolate yourself.

Low self-esteem, a recent loss, loneliness, and feelings

---

* *Youth Suicide* Peck, M.L., Farberow, N.L., and Litman, R.E., eds., (New York: Springer Publishing Co., 1985.)

of helplessness and hopelessness are the most common causes of suicidal depression. If you know someone who fits this profile, ask them if they need help, and help them get it.

Very often, depressed people are embarrassed and ashamed; they think that asking for help is admitting that they are inadequate wimps; that asking for help is the last resource of the crazy and the emotionally ill. That is not true. *Everyone* needs help in this life, sooner or later. It takes some of us longer to find it out.

College is the door to the big leagues, and what coaches are to sports, counselors are to life. They can't hit the ball for you, but if you've been striking out lately, they can help you modify your swing. Don't underestimate the value of a sympathetic, trained and knowledgeable professional.

This chapter will not take the place of a counselor, and may not be effective if you are already depressed. But you should know about the causes of depression to help you take care of yourself, to keep you from getting depressed.

To Prevent Depression . . .

To prevent depression in college, here are some basic, commonsense things you can do.

Be aware. Be aware that depression is common in college students. Not everyone will become depressed; but you can reduce the chances by taking care of yourself. With the suicide rate among teenagers and young adults rising so sharply, it is only reasonable to be informed.

Stay in touch with your family. Talk to them. They are important for you; don't cut yourself off from them.

When you came to college, you left your family, your friends, and all your usual, normal, day-to-day activities behind. Homesickness is common, and some depression is a normal element of homesickness. Separation often leaves a bleeding wound, that takes a while to heal. During this time, you need all the emotional support you can get.

Don't tie your self-worth to your grades. Hard work never killed anyone. Tying your self-worth to your grades, does. Depression, low grades, and low self-esteem form a vicious circle. If you do tie your self-worth to your grades, you are only as good as your last exam, and you can count on getting depressed whenever your last grade is lower than you hoped. When you're depressed, it's hard to study. Then your grades get worse, and your self-esteem goes down further. Around and around you go.

I know you are concerned with your parents' opinions; you want good grades so that they will think well of you. But that is too heavy a load for you to carry. Of course your parents want you to do well; all parents do. But you must understand that most well-adjusted parents will think well of you and love you no matter what grades you get, and that you can think well of yourself no matter what grades you get. Do not misinterpret their ambition for you to get good grades as a condition for love. If you don't believe this, you owe it to yourself and to them to check this out with them.

Don't take the responsibility for your parents' troubles. An important source of depression is the trouble parents might be having, emotional, financial, or perhaps even getting along with each other. Of course, if your parents are having troubles, you are probably concerned. You might, on some level, feel responsible. Confront that feeling of responsibility for your parents. In most cases, there is absolutely nothing you can do to improve their situation. Don't even think of trying. Sadness for your parents' unhappiness is an appropriate feeling; self-blame and depression are not. The best thing you can do, for yourself and them, is to not get in the way, offer your love and interest, and get on with your own life. Learn from their mistakes, and try to make different ones.

Work on making a new support system for yourself. I use the word "work" advisedly; it can sometimes be very hard to do. You may have to suffer rejections, sometimes a lot of them, before you create a group of new friends who will be open, supportive, and accepting, and with whom you can share your feelings and pains. And listen to them, also. Don't wait for them to get in touch with you; take an active part in forming and maintaining a network of friends. Call them and return their calls promptly. Give compliments freely. Enjoy your friends, and use them, but be there for them, also. Learn interdependence.

You may have to make yourself go out and find people. Depressed people are often isolated, and avoid contact with others. They may believe that others do not like them, and sometimes make it come true, a self-fulfilling prophecy, and see it as further proof of their worthlessness.

So go out and make things happen. The harder it is to motivate yourself, the more important it is that you go out and smile at people, ask how they are, and express an interest in their response. You need to do this for yourself. And when they invite you to an activity, go.

You can survive your first college love affair. In the early months of school, you may fill the void you felt on leaving home with a relationship with another person. Although this feels very good, it will leave you in a vulnerable position. Chances are your first relationship will not be your last. It may run a short course. When it ends, you may experience the worst loneliness and depression of your life. You may believe that you will never, ever have another such relationship. It may be a painful and stormy period for you.

Such an experience may leave you with a cynical attitude toward relationships. College years are often a time of temporary, shifting, shallow relationships. You may be more willing than most to establish a good, solid relationship, and you may find yourself disappointed many times. The morning-after cup of coffee is often bitter. The main problem is an expectation that people should be different than they are at this time of their lives. In fact, there is an atmosphere of experimentation that leads to many, short relationships. It is hard to be open to people, yet suspicious of them, at the same time. But it is sad to get "tough" too soon. Don't stop giving people a chance.

Periodically, review and revise your expectations. There are other expectations and hopes that may be disappointed. You may have unrealistic expectations that all your teachers should be good teachers, and interested in you personally; that courses should be more interesting; that grades should be higher, and that life should be more satisfying. The world is almost certainly not going to be the way you thought it should be. You have three choices: to adjust your expectations; to change the world; or to get angry or depressed. This is a problem that has occupied philosophers and psychologists for many years without resolution. Perhaps you know George Bernard Shaw's observation: "Reasonable men adapt themselves to the world. Unreasonable men adapt the world to themselves. Therefore all progress comes from unreasonable men." And you probably have seen or heard the prayer, "Give me the strength to change what can be changed, the patience to endure what cannot be changed, and the wisdom to know the difference."

After a loss, grieve, and go on. Very often, a loss of some kind precedes depression. The loss can be of a relative, an important relationship, economic security (a loan didn't come through), self-esteem (you may have flunked an exam, and begun to doubt your ability), or the esteem of others. Depression following a loss often includes the belief that what you lost was necessary for happiness. That is never, never true. What *is* necessary is to do your grieving, and to then get on with life, and the filling of your needs elsewhere.

Take charge of your life. Establish a sense of independence, self-reliance, and responsibility for yourself. Look at the areas in which you can take charge of your life and make your own decisions, i.e., how much to study, where to live, when it is good for you to go out, and with whom. Take charge of your life. Don't let yourself be a "victim," or believe you have no choice.

Recognize that you are a survivor, that no matter what the world throws at you, you will be able to manage, and very well too. You can deal with unpleasant situations. Your security lies, not in people making things easy for you, but within you, and your innate ability to land on your feet, or, if you fail, to get up, brush yourself off, and go on.

Accept your feelings. Accept your feelings, and yourself for having them. Whether loneliness, frustration, disappointment, anger, or feelings of inadequacy, don't think you shouldn't have these feelings, or that there is something wrong with you for having them. And don't hide them.

When you are at an impasse in your life, you may feel helpless and angry. Helpless anger can become depression. When, in spite of anger, needs are not met, the angry person may "give up," and their anger goes underground, turns inward, and converts to depression. Scratch a depressed student, and you will often find helpless, impotent rage beneath the surface. Sometimes the depression feels better than the anger. However, bringing the anger out is important, even though it may temporarily feel more painful, and the impotent rage that ensues may be difficult to channel.

Make sure you talk to someone about these feelings; get them out in the open; ventilate them.

Know your needs, and fill them. Be clear about what your needs are. Make up a plan that will fill them. Review your strategies for meeting your needs, discard those that aren't working for you, and try others. You don't have to meet all your needs, fully, all the time; but don't postpone meeting them too long, either.

For your physical needs, get enough sleep and rest, adequate nutrition, and enough exercise. Don't abuse your body with drugs. You need good physical health to cope with college and enjoy it.

Be assertive. Learn assertiveness in expressing your thoughts, feelings, and needs to others, without aggressiveness or manipulation, and without undue anxiety about the consequences. Such self-expression is necessary for your self-esteem, and for getting your important needs met.

It is ultimately up to you to fill your own needs. Others

can help, but this is a responsibility you can't delegate. You, and you alone, are in charge of taking care of yourself. Other people may be necessary, but it is up to you to find them. Don't take a passive position, of waiting for people to get around to you. Don't wait to be rescued.

Review your day every evening. Review your day every evening, and as you do, acknowledge yourself as a good, worthwhile person who did the best you knew how, who made decisions that seemed the best at the time. You may be your own severest critic; but if so, also be your own best friend. Accept your mistakes and failures, and like yourself anyway. Make peace with what you see as faults or deficiencies. Work with what you have, and who you are, and you will do well. Start from where you are, and go on.

Express your "right brain" functions. Express *both* sides of your brain. Of course, train your left brain functions of logical, sequential thought, but also express your right brain functions through, for example, art and poetry. Explore yourself fearlessly, and express what you find creatively and with pride. Keep a journal in which you draw or color, and then write, your feelings, even when they are sad. Some sadness, like joy, is a normal part of life.

Finally, when things are going badly (as they sometimes will), reassure yourself that

- you are still a good person
- you are indeed competent
- there are and always will be people who love you
- and that this too will pass.

And call your conseling service, especially if you are ever considering permanent solutions to temporary problems.

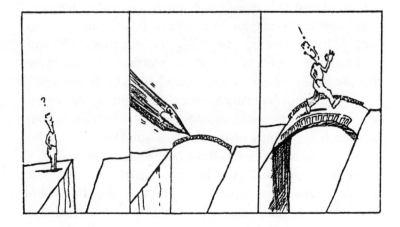

13 Creative Coping

lbert Einstein said, "Imagination is more important than knowledge."

Whatever man can imagine, man can do. Creativity is the key which can unlock the universe and your life. Creativity is the pathway by which we may just possibly overcome mankind's very real problems, and reach the future.

Not everyone thinks creativity is so great. New, different, unique ideas are not welcome everywhere. Of course, just because ideas are new does not necessarily make them better; not everything new is an advance. But also, many people are comfortable with the answers they already have, and don't want to hear about your solutions. Some answers that seem fine to you will rub a lot of people the wrong way.

Steve Wozniak, a drop-out from college, was working for a major "main-frame" computer manufacturer when he made and programmed a small personal computer, which he gave away at first to his friends. When he offered his computer to his employer, it was rejected. He then went ahead to found the Apple Computer Company and the whole personal computer industry. Later, rich and famous, he returned to Berkeley under an assumed name to finish his undergraduate degree. There an electrical engineering instructor who did not recognize him rejected his novel solutions to a problem, telling him to do it his, the instructor's, way. This struck my son (also an electrical engineering student), and all the students who knew who he really was, as hilarious. They asked, "If 'Woz' had taken this course first, would he have invented the personal computer?"

Coping does not mean that someone is going to show you the answers to problems. Coping means learning to find your own answers. Creative coping is, more than anything else, a state of mind. Before we talk further about it, let's see if we can demonstrate it.

EXERCISE 13. Crossing a Chasm.

Purpose: To explore the process of creative problem solving.

Method: Seat yourself comfortably at a table, preferably in a group. In front of you have a sheet of blank paper, and some felt-tipped pens. Imagine yourself having to cross a chasm. You have any and every tool available under the sun. Draw your solution. Do not read further until after you have finished.

Comment: After you have finished, share your drawn solution with the other participants. Were there as many solutions as people? Stay in touch with your feelings as you look at the myriad bridges, helicopters, rockets, etc. which others used in getting over the gorge. What did you learn about yourself? Was your plan solid and realistic, or did you use fantasy and imagination? How creative and imaginative did you allow yourself to be? Did you act spontaneously, or carefully? Did you have more than one way of getting across? Would your plan work? Would your bridge hold up, would you make it across? Was this exercise just another evaluation of your ability, or was it a fun experience, an enjoyable challenge?

Now, repeat the exercise. This time, if your first solution was totally practical and realistic, allow yourself the luxury of letting your fantasy go, and find the wildest and most unrealistic solution that presents itself to your mind. If, on the other hand, your first solution was totally impractical, unrealistic, unsafe, and unworkable, then repeat it looking for something a little more connected to reality. Did you learn what your problem-solving style is?

Fantasy vs. Reality

As in most things, there is something good about both approaches. College classes often stress the known, the practical and specific. Even, sometimes, in what should be the arts, they get technical and specific. The practical and specific is important, and fine as part of a balanced program. However, if the creative, expressive, emotive aspect is missing from your courses, you may have to supply the balance. At this stage in your life, I would encourage you to promote the use of fantasy. It is an important part of creativity. You will have plenty of time later to adapt your fantasies to reality.

What are creative people like?

Creativity Requires Unconventional Thinking

Creative people display unconventional thinking, sensitivity, and independence. That can sometimes be hard for teenagers and even young adults, who are struggling for peer acceptance. Even worse, since both sexes often see sensitivity as a feminine virtue, and independence as a masculine trait, the creative boy may appear more effeminate to his peers, and the creative girl more masculine. (Ohmigod! How awful!)

Creative people often abandon old ways of thinking, so that they seem to think differently from other people. This is almost a sure way for creative people to get "in trouble" with some teachers.

Creative people are less likely to suppress their own uncomfortable ideas, and are more willing to explore their own fantasy and subconscious. When they express their ideas, and especially when they act on them, they can withstand the disapproval and shock of others. They regard their freedom of thought and action as essential to their creativity. They are often, in their zeal, provocative and inflammatory.

Can creativity be fostered and taught? Or are creative people just naturally creative?

A religious teaching organization in California once sponsored a conference to explore why their people had so few Nobel prizes. A friend of mine attended the conference, and reported that they agreed that creativity was encouraged by freedom of thought and a questioning attitude, but that creativity was less important to them than accepting the truths of the bible as they interpreted it. They decided they preferred their truth to Nobel prizes.

If creativity can be encouraged by an atmosphere of freedom of thought and action, and a questioning attitude, it can also be discouraged by an attempt to insist on conformity of thought and belief.

Paul Torrance, a Georgia educator who teaches teachers how to teach, compiled this amazing list of the characteristics of highly creative people, by combining studies that are in the literature on creativity. No one, of course, has all these qualities, but creative people have many of them.

Characteristics of Creative People

Accepts disorder
Strong affection
Awareness of others
Attracted to mysterious
Bashful outwardly
Courageous
Defies conventions of
  courtesy
Desires to excel
Differentiated
  value-hierarchy
Disturbs organization
Emotional
Energetic
Doesn't fear being
  thought "different"
Full of curiosity
Likes solitude
Independence in thinking
Intuitive
Introverted
Lacks social graces
Never bored
Not hostile or
  negativistic
Oddities of habit
Becomes preoccupied
  with a problem
Questioning
Receptive to external
  stimuli
Regresses occasionally
Rejection of repression
Resolute
Self-starter
Self-confident

Sense of destiny
Sensitive to beauty
Sincere
Speculative
Strives for distant goals
Temperamental
Tender emotions
Thorough
Somewhat uncultured,
  primitive
Unwilling to accept
  anything on mere
  say-so
Versatile
Somewhat withdrawn
  and quiescent
Adventurous
Altruistic
Always baffled by
  something
Attempts difficult jobs
  (sometimes too
  difficult)
Constructive in criticism
Deep and conscientious
  convictions
Defies conventions of
  health
Determination
Discontented
Dominant (not in power
  sense)
Emotionally sensitive
A fault-finder
Feels whole parade is out
  of step

Appears haughty and
self-satisfied at times
Independence in
judgment
Individualistic
Industrious
Keeps unusual hours
Makes mistakes
Nonconforming
Not popular
Persistent
Preference for complex
ideas
Radical
Receptive to the ideas of
others
Rejection of suppression
as a mechanism of
impulse control
Reserved
Self-assertive
Self-aware
Self-sufficient
Sense of humor
Shuns power
Not interested in small
details
Spirited in disagreement
Stubborn
Tenacious
Timid
Unconcerned about
power
Unsophisticated, naive
Visionary
Willing to take risks

Creative People May Not be Valued

What a fascinating list. They add up to a willingness to explore, and a resistance to conformity. Creativity follows. As you can see, such a person might not be too popular with teachers, or even other students. College administrators and teachers can have a difficult time with young people who are exploring their own potential and creativity. In spite of some obviously good qualities, such a person might not feel valued, even by his classmates (except, perhaps, by a discerning few).

Two Functions of the Brain

Kekule was the German chemist who, in 1865, formulated the "ring" theory of the constitution of benzene, which the Encyclopedia Britannica calls the "most brilliant piece of prediction to be found in the whole range of organic chemistry." He recounts that he visualized this formula one evening when, as he dozed in front of a fire, he dreamed of snakes biting their own tails and thus forming loops.

Albert Einstein once asked a friend, "Why is it I get my best ideas in the morning while I am shaving?"

At the time, there was no answer. Now we know why. The mysterious, ineffable workings of creativity now lend themselves to examination. It is perhaps easiest to understand if we look first at two opposite functions of the brain.

In 1982 Roger Sperry received the Nobel Prize for demonstrating that there are two "sides" to us.

The Left and Right Brains

We all have two hemispheres of our brain, left and right. The right hemisphere contains the motor and sensory areas that control the left side of the body. The left hemisphere contains the areas that control the right side of the body, and also contains the speech center that controls the ability to talk and write. (Even in left-handed people, the speech center is generally in the left hemisphere.) These verbal skills are responsible for what we commonly think of as intelligence: the ability to think logically and sequentially, to analyze, to evaluate, and to come to rational conclusions. These are the skills most highly valued in college. Without words, we are almost helpless in this verbal world.

People who have a stroke or tumor or injury involving the left brain motor area become paralyzed on the right side of the body. If the injury involves the speech area, they also become incapable of communicating. Until Sperry, most doctors and psychologists thought that the right brain was only a pale image of the left, controlling the left side of the body, but without the speech ability, and not doing much else. In fact, very often strokes and injuries to the right brain that avoided the motor area were not noticed. If people weren't paralyzed on the left side of the body, no one knew to even look for any other effects.

The Right Brain Functions

What Sperry discovered is that the right brain has its own unique abilities that are different from those of the left brain. He found that the right brain is the *superior* hemisphere for all the nonverbal, nonmathematical, and nonsequential tasks. It is better than the left brain at interpreting space and images. It is better at visual and nonvisual imagery.

You may be interested in the story of how he discovered this.

It started with Joseph Bogen, a neurosurgeon in Los Angeles, who devised an operation for epilepsy. One form of epilepsy is characterized by "grand mal" seizures; that is, an electrical stimulus starts in one part of the brain, spreads over that hemisphere, then passes through the corpus callosum that connects the two hemispheres, and spreads over the second hemisphere. When that happens, the afflicted person has a convulsion. Although an occasional convulsion causes no harm, some people have them as many as twenty-five times in a day, and cannot control them with medication. Such people have a great risk of eventually developing brain damage.

Dr. Bogen reasoned that if the corpus callosum were cut, the electrical impulse could not spread to the second hemisphere, and therefore a convulsion would not occur. With the consent of his patients, he did this operation, and found that they did indeed stop having convulsions.

About six months after the first such patient's operation, Bogen was watching a psychologist administer an I.Q. test to him. This particular I.Q. test included a section that timed how quickly a person could match designs using blocks. He noticed that the patient's hands seemed to be "fighting each other," and asked him to sit on his right hand. The left hand, connected to the right brain, performed the task quickly and easily. Then he asked the patient to sit on his left hand. The right hand, connected to the left brain, could not get the pattern right! Being a neurosurgeon, he enlisted the help of Dr. Sperry, a researcher who had already done some studies on split-brain cats.

To study these split-brain patients, Dr. Sperry used a tachistoscope to flash information that would reach only one hemisphere and not the other. The tachistoscope is an instrument that flashes a picture or a word so briefly that it disappears before the eye can move. Knowing the anatomy of the eye, the picture or word can be flashed to a part of the retina that leads to only one hemisphere or the other.

Then, using multiple choice questions, he asked the

person to respond to the information, either by words, or by pointing. When they responded with words or their right hand, they could only use the information that had been supplied to the left brain. And they used only their right hemisphere when they pointed with their left hand.

In my favorite experiment, reported by Michael Gazzaniga, he showed a picture of a snow scene to the right brain, and of a chicken claw to the left brain. He asked, "What goes with what you saw?" The multiple choice answers included a shovel and a rooster. With the right hand, connected to the left brain, the patient picked out the rooster (to go with the chicken claw). With the left hand, connected to the right brain, he picked out the snow shovel (to go with the snow scene). So far, so good. But then he aked the patient, "Why did you pick out the rooster and the shovel? Now, his left brain, containing the speech center, had not seen the snow scene, and did not know why the right brain had picked out the shovel. So he said, "Well, the rooster goes with the chicken claw . . ." and added, without missing a beat, "and the shovel is to shovel out the chicken coop, of course!"

The left brain is seldom at a loss for words to explain what it has seen, even when it doesn't know what it is talking about. Does this sound familiar to you?

On the basis of many similar experiments, Sperry found that the right brain is better than the left brain at the following specific tasks:

1. Reading faces. That is, the right brain is better at recognizing faces, and interpreting the emotions that are being projected.

2. Discriminating and recalling nondescript shapes. That is, if a shape is relatively formless (a rock, for example), the right brain can still reproduce it; the left brain can't.

3. The intuitive perception and understanding of geometric principles. This is what Dr. Bogen first noticed that made him realize that the two brains are different. For example, the right brain can quickly direct the left hand to draw a simple stick house. The right hand directed by the left brain draws the correct number of lines, but can't attach them to look like a house!

4. Discriminating musical chords. When two or more notes are played together, the right brain can tell you which notes are being played and can reproduce them. The left brain can't.

5. Fitting designs into larger forms. That is, the right brain can pick a specific form out of a larger overall pattern. The left brain can't.

6. Perceiving wholes from a collection of parts (the so-called gestalt function). Given several unconnected patterns, the right brain can assemble them into a meaningful shape. The left brain can't.

Isn't it amazing that all these functions can be lost in a right brain stroke, and nobody even *notices?* And most people, even those who know the split-brain patients well, can't even tell that they have had such major surgery. As long as the left brain can talk and be plausible, everybody thinks they are normal. What does that tell you about our world, and our educational system?

The Two Brains Work Together

In his Nobel Prize acceptance speech, Sperry said, "In the normal state, the two hemispheres appear to work closely together as a unit. . . . One beneficial outcome that appears to hold up is an enhanced awareness, in education and elsewhere, of the important role of nonverbal components and forms of intellect. . . . The whole world of inner experience (the world of the humanities), long rejected by twentieth-century scientific materialism, thus becomes recognized and included within the domain of science."

We Begin to Understand Creativity

We now know that images and fantasy begin in the right brain. They are so-called "right-brain" functions. The ability to see images in clouds, to fantasize events and outcomes, to experience altered states of consciousness, are all demonstrated to involve right brain activity more than left. We can demonstrate this by electrical activity and blood flow studies. When you daydream or fantasize or listen to music or remember colors, blood flow shifts from the left to the right brain, and the electrical activity of the right brain increases.

The ability to see patterns, make gestalts and come to likely conclusions on the basis of a few facts is also a right brain function. It may be what we call "intuition."

The two hemispheres normally interconnect through a broad band of 200 million nerve fibers called the corpus callosum. The left brain therefore has the opportunity to look at these right brain productions immediately, and to evaluate them, compare them with logical reality, and organize them effectively. The left brain is in charge of deciding whether these images are practical, and if so is responsible for using and expressing them effectively. It doesn't do much good to have marvelous fantasies if they just remain fantasies. You have to *do* something with them if they are to be of any value. Is it still true in the morning? Will it work? If it does, then go with it! Do it! *Make* it work! You know, creativity is ten percent inspiration and ninety percent perspiration. It doesn't do any good to think or know something, if you don't or can't follow through on it. Leonardo DaVinci said the "supreme misfortune is when theory outstrips performance."

The Creative Person Uses Both Sides of the Brain

Creativity, then, is the result of an interplay between the right and left hemispheres. It begins in the right hemisphere. Too much left hemisphere influence at the beginning, too much realism, organization, evaluation and critical judgment can stifle creativity before it gets started. For creativity to function, the left hemisphere activity must, for a while at least, be suspended, in order to allow the right hemisphere to do its work. Then, the left hemisphere must interact with the right hemisphere imagery and fantasy in order to create something useful and workable. Too little left hemisphere function lets the fantasy and imagery dissipate in pleasant but unproductive activity.

All Children are Creative

If you do not feel creative, when did you lose it? You were certainly creative as a child. All children are creative.

Given a little bit of sand or a few crayons, children immediately create fantasies. A toy in a big box is often less exciting to them than the box it came in; the box has more possibilities. Children love puzzles and problems to be solved.

Believing there is a right way and a wrong way of thinking inhibits our imagination and suppresses our creativity. The best way to become creative again is to allow your right brain the freedom to express itself freely, to enjoy what you find, and to use it to solve your problems.

There are blocks to this process. There are social blocks; as I noted, some creative behaviors are not highly regarded socially. There are personal blocks; you may not feel secure enough about yourself to allow your right brain to function freely. And there are left brain blocks; anything that doesn't seem to make immediate logical sense is open to ridicule. These powerful blocks stand in the way of creativity. You have to explore yourself and remove these blocks to again experience your own creative energy. Here are some keys you can use to release your creativity.

Think well of yourself. Your creative endeavor comes from within, and requires enjoying who you are. To be creative, you must think well enough of yourself to enjoy your right brain processes. A good way to avoid being creative is to deprecate yourself. If you don't especially care for the way you are, you aren't going to be receptive to your own creative thoughts.

Be willing to be different. "Different" is often "better." Creativity means doing something that hasn't been done before. Trying to be like others will make you a clone. You can't copy creativity. Respecting authorities and trying to do the "right thing" has its own special virtues, but can inhibit innovation.

Don't fear criticism. Use criticism when appropriate, but be able to ignore it when it is not. When you have a new idea, you might think that people will say, "How wonderful!" Actually, it doesn't happen that way too often. More frequently, people will think, "How awful!" Anything new invites disapproval. Very few things of real value were appreciated at first. Most innovations are greeted with cat-calls. Stravinsky's "The Firebird" caused a riot, and the first impressionist painters were refused exhibition space by the established artists.

The person who must appreciate and approve of what you have done is you. Relying on the criticism or approval of others is the royal road to mediocrity.

Let creativity be its own reward. Creative effort brings its own reward in pleasure, with fame and fortune incidental. Working for material rewards often means shaping your efforts too much to please others. Working for material rewards has been the downfall of many an innovator. Rely on the thrill of discovery, the solid satisfaction of innovation, and the enjoyment of finding new frontiers.

Creativity may mean to work alone. Creativity is often a solitary occupation. What you do, you must do alone, at least your part in it. You can certainly build on and use the efforts of those who went before you. Only a few things were totally new, or developed in a vacuum. You can bounce ideas off others, and be stimulated by them. You can also use the efforts of others.

For example, nuclear fission was discovered in 1938 by two Germans, O. Hahn and F. Strassmann, when, building on the work of Fermi and others, they bombarded uranium with neutrons and created barium. That was creative. To bring this discovery to fruition required the cooperative efforts of many creative people. It was communicated by two refugees, Meitner and Frisch, to Nils Bohr, a Danish physicist, who came to the U.S. and communicated it to Einstein, who brought it to the attention of Roosevelt, who asked Oppenheimer to oversee the Manhattan project. To make atomic fission workable needed the help of many people and much money. But the creative work was done by individuals, each taking and working on a part of the problem. Many of the individuals never knew the big picture.

Have you read *The Soul of a New Machine?* A book about the development of a new computer, it showed how the combined effort of dozens of people succeeded because the project manager allowed the individuals involved to do their part without hindrance, in their own time, in their own way. When the computer was finished, the company management broke up the group because they didn't like all that individuality. When committees try to be creative, they rarely succeed. A camel is a horse that was designed by a committee. Don't be afraid to work by yourself.

Don't compare yourself with others. Competition and worrying about what or who is better is death to creativity. Creativity can't be measured on a scale, or compared with the efforts of others. The product is not the issue. A child painting a horse, or your finding a new solution to a problem in physics, can be as original, as unique, as satisfying, as Picasso painting a picture of the women in his life. The process of creativity does not depend on, and cannot be measured by, the product. The value of what you produce may be argued over for centuries by historians and auctioneers; but the degree of creativity displayed is not measurable on any scale yet devised.

Allow all your feelings, good and bad. Feelings, good and bad, are an integral part of creativity. Bad feelings may be the source of inspiration, as good feelings may reward it. Furthermore, the creative effort itself is painful and frustrating as it gropes toward fruition. An unfeeling environment is sterile.

Experience the timelessness of the "here-and-now." There is a shift in consciousness when you are being creative that focuses you so intensely that you can lose track of time. Hours can become minutes. Time disappears. There is an immediacy in creativity that collapses time. Have you experienced this? If the outside world intrudes, you can "lose your concentration," and become aware again of what time it is.

A Framework
for Understanding the Mysterious

It seems clear that the workings of the right brain, the province of the psychobiologist (Sperry is a psychobiologist), are the same stuff which so intrigue poets, Eastern philosophers, artists, dancers, and physicists. Sperry concluded in his Nobel acceptance speech, "A unifying new interpretive framework emerges with far-reaching impact not only for science but for those ultimate value-belief guidelines by which mankind has tried to live and find meaning."

Translated, this means that it is the *interaction* of the right and left brain functions that determines creativity in and appreciation of music, art, science, thought, beauty, color, and design. Isabel Briggs-Myers, co-author of the Myers-Briggs test that measures Jungian types, says, "Among research scientists and design engineers . . . their greatest gifts come directly from their intuition—the flashes of inspiration, the insight into relationships of ideas and meaning of symbols, the imagination, the originality, the access to resources of the unconscious, the ingenuity, and the visions of what could be."

Imagery is the Tool of Creativity

We all use imagery when we dream and when we create. Imagery is not only visual (though that is its most common meaning); it is also sensual, kinesthetic, emotional, intellectual, and spiritual. Imagery may be mankind's best hope; our future may be unlimited because we can imagine what we would like it to be. Using imagery, we can explore ourselves, others, the universe, and beyond. Imagery serves as a vehicle for bringing our nonverbal inner experiences and our nonverbal knowledge to awareness. However, for us to be creative, we must expose that imagery to our sense of logic and reason.

Seeing and Drawing Your Images

Do you have, or do you know someone with, math anxiety? Well, art anxiety is just like it. When called upon to draw something, people often become anxious. They freeze into immobility, humiliated by their earlier memories and experiences about their inadequacy, knowing they had no "talent" or "originality." To help shore up your suddenly collapsed self-esteem, begin by anchoring a good feeling (see Exercise 7) and use the good feelings it produces.

Now, for just a little while, we're going to fake out that critical, evaluative left brain by a "nonsense" exercise.

EXERCISE 14. Creative Imagery

Purpose: To learn to see and draw your inner images.
Method. For this exercise you will need drawing material. Place some clean paper, about 8 by 11 or 11 by 17, on a table or the floor, and have coloring materials available (broad-tipped felt pens, soft pastels). Put on some music; anything you like as long as it is slow. Listening to music is a right-brain activity. Then, after you read this paragraph, shut your eyes and, with the fingers of your dominant hand, feel different parts of yourself; for example, your hair, your skin, your clothing. At the same time, using your non-dominant hand, make marks on the paper that represent the feel of what you are touching. Make marks that tell what the music sounds like. Make happy marks. Make sad marks. What does anger look like? Make marks that sound like rain, and like thunder.

Open your eyes, and look at what you have drawn. You didn't make the marks deliberately and you made them with your "wrong" hand, so you can relieve yourself from criticism; you aren't "responsible" for them. Turn the paper round and round, and look at it, sideways and upside down. Take your pastels and felt tips and begin to add color. Keep looking at what you've drawn and turn it, coloring as you go. You will see something that triggers an image or a memory. Keep looking for these images. *Bring out an image* with your colors. Keep coloring for about ten or fifteen minutes, or until you feel finished. Keep the music going; it is important, as is not talking while you are drawing.

It's nice to enjoy what you have done, but don't laugh at yourself too much; suspend your critical judgment about the aesthetic value of your efforts. Instead, write a fantasy or free or rhymed verse about your creation. You may want to make it a fable by starting with "Once upon a time . . ." or you may indulge in "automatic writing" where you write one word, which suggests another, and another. Imagine being what you have created and write a story about what you would do and feel as this creation. Remember, it is important to suspend your critical faculties, and to write for your eyes alone. This is your secret fantasy and you needn't share it with a soul. Write ten lines or more. Read your story to yourself. How does it feel to be creating your own fantasy?

Now after a few minutes look at your creation from still another perspective. Does the story you created talk about you symbolically? Is the story you wrote about you? Is it a metaphor for what is going on with you? Does it have anything to do with what is happening in your life right now? It was you who found the images; where did these images and your fairy tale come from?

Comment: Anything can be used as material from which you can create an image: clouds, random remarks by other people, a musical phrase, a suggestive movement, something you read, random marks you create on a piece of paper. Leonardo DaVinci said, "I cannot forbear to mention . . . a new device for study which, although it may seem trivial, is nevertheless extremely useful in arousing the mind to various inventions. And this is, when you look at a wall spotted with stains . . . you may discover a resemblance to various landscapes, beautified with mountains, rivers, rocks, trees . . . or again you may see battles and figures in action, or strange faces and costumes and an endless variety of objects which you could reduce to complete and well-drawn forms. And these appear on such wall confusedly, like the sound of bells in whose jangle you may find any name or word you choose to imagine."

More important, the image you create comes from within you, and relates to your situation, your experience, your knowledge. Moreover, it may be information that is not readily accessible to you in any other way.

You are now an Artist

There are two general ways to use this information. You can use it to create something of value: artwork, theories, inventions, books. What you create will have come from, and be a part of, you. Have you ever noticed the affection and defensiveness that people have toward their own creations? When you criticize someone's theory or work of art, they react as if you were attacking their child!

On the other hand, you can use it as information about *you.* In a very real sense, your images give you information about you that you often cannot obtain in any other way, at least not as easily—information that can be extremely helpful in coping with your life. There is a lot of information about you tucked away in your brain, including things you learned before you had words to attach to them. Do you remember how a fragrance can recall Grandma's house? You can recall them through the arts as well.

EXERCISE 15. Two Animals

Purpose: To learn more about yourself.

Method: Make some stray marks on a piece of paper. One way is to dip some kite string into ink and drag it across paper, now this way, now that. As you look at it, look for two animals. That's right, find two different animals in the marks you have created. Turn the paper around until you see them. When you see them, color them so that you bring them out. Then, on a separate piece of paper, write three adjectives for each animal that best describe how they look to you. Then write a conversation that might take place between these two animals about some problem or concern that is bothering you these days. What would they say to each other about this? Write a page of dialogue.

Comment: Almost invariably, these two animals will represent two different parts of you, and they will present two different sides of the problem. It may be surprising to you how well they present their cases. For example, you may see a turtle and a bird. The turtle may be slow, persistent, dull. The bird may be beautiful, soaring, and free. The turtle may say, "One step at a time." The bird may say, "Come on, let's fly!" The turtle will respond, "No, I have to study." Bird: "Stick in the mud! Life is passing you by!" Turtle: "You go ahead; I'll catch up."

You may think, "You know, that's exactly what's going through my mind right now. How did they know?" How did *who* know? That was *you* talking! This will give you the opportunity to see both sides of a conflict at once, and so make a decision that may have room for both your animals.

Right Brain People
In A Left Brain World

I have stressed the importance of integrating the right and left brain functions, and using them appropriately. It is inefficient to solve logical problems with the right brain. It is equally inefficient to approach nonlogical functions with the left brain.

Some people who try to solve all their problems with the left brain miss much of the pleasure in life. On the other hand, people who get lost in fantasy can also have trouble coping with the real world. Although "right-brain people" have great imagination and really enjoy certain aspects of life, they may have difficulty meeting their goals. People say they have trouble "finding themselves."

The right brain functions are pleasurable and fun. The right brain is the source of fantasy and imagination. You are in your right brain when you are playing a sport superbly and everything is landing where it should; when you surrender to music and dance; when you are in that

altered state of consciousness induced by a little marijuana or beer; when you are meditating, or lost in sex or
art. Children are in their right brain when they are playing. The right brain functions carry their own reinforcers;
they feel so good that you want to do them over and over.

However, play by children is never just right brain activity; it is always a combination of left and right. For
example, children don't just play in the sand; they play
in the sand and build a sand castle. They ride on a little
tricycle and pretend they are race car drivers. They play
with crayons and finger paints, and say they have drawn
a picture of themselves doing something (often difficult to
see until they have pointed it out).

Using the Right Brain Creatively

They are *using* their right brain functions creatively,
and as they do, they learn to use and enjoy their left brain
functions as well. Play, it is said, is the work of children.

Parents who mean well but don't understand this process often minimize and rush it. Then they tell the child,
do something *useful!* Don't just amuse yourself; get to
work! Do your homework! Carry out the trash! Johnny,
rake the lawn. Mary, vacuum the rugs. Don't dawdle.
Come on, now, stop playing.

Children get very confused about these messages. They
never can work as well or as long or as hard or as efficiently
as their parents or teachers think they should, unless they
give up their play. They come to "understand" that play
is fun and bad and work is not fun and good. Some give
up their fun, especially older children, and become re-

sponsible, hardworking, serious, unhappy perfectionists. Others learn to hate the call to work, and secretly feel inadequate because they like to play. Most probably learn that there is work and there is play, and sometimes you do one and sometimes you do the other; you have a nine to five job, and then you enjoy yourself. Very few people actually learn how to combine the two so that they enjoy their work. Most of those who do manage to enjoy their work, do so by making a living out of their play, by becoming musicians, or actors, or professional athletes.

To make play out of work, you must first accept your right-brain imagination, fantasy, intuition, and originality for the gift it is. Too many of us put ourselves down for these gifts. They are great! They may not be appreciated by others; but it is really O.K. for you to feel good about your imagination, and about yourself.

Then, as you learn the nuts-and-bolts facts you have to know, for exams and for life, use your imagination to see these facts in new and exciting ways. Play with them. Think, "What if . . ." Make pictures and color them. Use both sides of your brain when studying. Be creative. Read the lines, and between them. It will add pleasure to your studies, and improve your memory logarithmically.

Then apply both sides of your brain to your own life, and your own problems. Be imaginative, and creative.

A very creative and sensitive young friend was told by many teachers in a prestigious art school that he was in danger of flunking out because his way of doing things was not practical or acceptable; he was too outlandish and independent. He worked very hard, however, and received support from just a couple of teachers, enough to persist in his outlandish technique. Now, still in his twenties, his unique work has appeared on the cover of several national magazines, including *Time, Fortune,* and *Rolling Stone,* and he has more work than he can handle.

Our colleges are of two minds about creativity. It is taught as a form of spectator sport; we study and admire the products of a few creative geniuses, but pay little attention to the actual creative process of the individual student. You will be rewarded for acquiring information, but not for fantasizing about what to do with it.

Creativity flourishes where it is nurtured, where the expressions of crazy fantasies, ridiculous ideas, and wild assumptions are encouraged, admired, and valued. The creative mind feeds on strange relationships, tolerance of disarray, and enough time for it all to gel. Although ultimately disorder must be ordered, we need a way of temporarily restraining the left hemisphere's goal-directed behavior and critical evaluation long enough for our other elusive hemisphere to speak. We must for a while surrender the feeling of being in charge.

Your left hemisphere will not willingly give up this control. Rollo May wrote, "My insight broke into my conscious mind *against what I had been trying to think rationally* . . . the unconscious broke through in opposition to the conscious belief to which I was clinging." Those who allow their fantasies free rein to interact with their rational abilities are rewarded by intuitive insights.

We Create Our Own Lives

We are all artists in the business of designing our own lives. We can accept the norms, ideas, and values of those around us, and become artistic hacks, or we can create our own inspired and inspiring lives. We can be in charge, and our tools can be our own creative power. We can become the person we dream.

Be creative; be stubborn; be outlandish sometimes. It's your life you are designing.

14 Pathways

The Dean of Student Affairs sighed when Raymond came in again as requested. He asked, "What's going on, Raymond?"

"I don't know what you mean," answered Raymond.

"Your grades keep dropping. Is something troubling you?"

"I just don't seem to be able to study."

"What do you want out of life, Raymond?"

"What do I want out of life?"

"Yes."

"I don't know what you mean."
"Why are you in college?"
"Well, my parents wanted me to come."
"Did you want to come?"
"Sure."
"Why?"
"Why?"
"Yes, why did you want to come to college?"
"To get a degree, I guess."
"Have you thought about taking a year or two off, and coming back later?"
"I hadn't thought about it."
"What do you think of that idea?"
"I don't think my parents would go for it. They want me to get a degree."
"What do *you* want, Raymond?"
"I don't know. I guess I want to get a degree too."
"And then?"
"Then?"
"Yes, then, after college."
"I don't know. I hadn't thought about it."

People with goals know where they are going and what they want to be, and it makes college much easier for them.

In Greek mythology, Heracles was given ten tasks to accomplish in order to achieve immortality. What tasks will you have to accomplish to achieve your goals?

Have you ever read *Siddhartha* by Herman Hesse? It chronicles the adventures of a young man who seeks to discover the meaning of his life. Each adventure teaches him a different lesson, and in the process the world unfolds to him with yet another meaning. In the end, as an old man, he is recognized as the Buddha.

You too have tasks you must achieve and lessons you

must learn, if you are to achieve your goals, and so have a reasonably enjoyable and satisfying life. (We're not even talking Buddha here.)

I have said that it is important to distinguish between two different types of goals. In prior chapters I talked about the basic needs people have: caring, individuation, self-esteem, dealing with their internalized critics, confidence, and self-expression, and said that in general, achieving goals that fill these needs leads to good feelings, and not achieving them leads to painful feelings. But you can't directly achieve these goals. There are paths you must travel, and tasks you must accomplish, in order to achieve these basic goals. You must first achieve a set of intermediate *pathway goals* which, being achieved, will ultimately lead to your basic goals.

Children play a game, "What do you want to be when you grow up?" College is a time of transition to real-life, now-it-counts, goals, and to the selection of pathways that you hope will lead to the satisfaction of your basic goals. These pathways convert aimless play into a journey with a purpose. You acquire a direction.

However, most students enter college at seventeen or eighteen, and many are just not ready to select realistic pathways for themselves. There is nothing wrong with that! Most of you will not know for several years yet what you really want or what to expect. You may try many courses and even several different majors before you find one you enjoy and in which you feel happy and successful. College should be a time when you can explore various fields, enjoy yourself, and let ideas percolate for a while. In the course of your explorations, something may interest you. Then you will have found a path and yourself.

So if it isn't happening yet, don't push it. I suggest you take some exploratory courses the first year or two, covering several different fields—history, English Literature, chemistry, psychology, art, biology—a "smattering." If nothing grabs you, if you do not find a "purpose" in college, there is nothing wrong with taking time out, perhaps working for a year or two. Many students are doing this now. Many students who have taken time out return with a purpose, and find school much more productive and interesting.

College is a time for measuring yourself, against yourself, against others, against the world. Here you get a realistic grasp of where and how far you can go. You glimpse your possibilities. For at least the next few years, you can overreach yourself and fall without paying heavy dues. Or, perhaps, you will surprise even yourself by how far, how fast, you can travel.

There is no way to tell in advance whether goals are realistic or not. All the great advances in life were considered unrealistic at first; that is the nature of great advances. The Wright brothers were considered impractical dreamers. You may be told not to aspire. I have had, among my better students in medical school, a 39-year-old woman who left a successful career as a singer, a man who had dropped out of college to be a carpenter for 7 years, a paraplegic, a man who could barely express himself in English, and many, many others who were told of some reason why they should not aspire to medical school. I myself was told that I was too *short* to be a doctor; people needed, I was told, a doctor they could look *up* to. So you see, you must take people's warnings with a grain of salt. If you have faith in yourself, go for it; do not settle for less, until you have given it your best shot. Otherwise, although you may have the satisfaction of achieving your goals, you may be disappointed with what you find.

A simple formula for success is:

Feeling good about yourself + enjoying what you do + mastery = more good feelings about yourself + more enjoyment + mastery = more good feelings about yourself + more enjoyment + mastery, etc.

An equally simple formula for failure is

Not feeling good about yourself + not enjoying what you do + failing = feeling worse about yourself + liking what you do even less + failing = feeling even worse about yourself + hating what you do + failing, etc., etc., etc.

These are self-perpetuating cycles. If you are doing well at something and you are getting pleasure from what you are doing and you feel good about yourself, then you will do well at it and enjoy it and feel good about yourself. If you are not doing well or you are not enjoying what you are doing or you don't feel good about yourself, you will do it badly and you will not get pleasure from it and you will not feel good about yourself.

Around and around we go. Be in charge of which merry-go-round you get on.

APPENDIX A
Keeping a Journal

The profoundly moving journals of Anne Frank, Anais Nin, and Virginia Woolf have revived an interest in journal-keeping of late, inspiring many to record and document their lives. Some other famous diarists include Samuel Pepys, Henry David Thoreau, Charles Darwin, and Sylvia Plath.

Psychologist Jan Rainwater writes, ''I see my journal as one 'place' that I can always go to work out a current problem, to wrestle into articulate awareness a current feeling or mood, to record the meaning of a recent experience, to come to a decision.''*

There is space in the back of the book for you to begin your journal. For a little while each day, take the time to write or draw whatever comes to mind.

Record your random drawings, and express your thoughts, images, and fantasies. If you make drawings of your images, feelings, thoughts, no matter how crude, you have captured them, and can remind yourself of them at your leisure. Writing a story about what you have drawn will bring out their meaning for you. It may keep you from making one-sided decisions. It may make it easier to find solutions with which all the different parts of you are comfortable.

Where and when should you draw and write in such a journal? First and foremost, *privately.* Such a journal is for your eyes only. If you draw and write knowing that others will see and read it, you may not feel comfortable allowing your imagination and feelings full rein. Your basic purpose in keeping such a journal is to explore, non-judgmentally, your inner images and thoughts.

What shall you draw and write about? Anything, everything. Doodle, make graffiti, smear your fingerprints, draw a picture of your teacher. Write a poem. Tell someone what you really think about them. Write dialogues with people. If there is some feeling churning inside or something happening in your life you can't let go of, let it out onto the paper.

Date your drawings and entries, and make a note of who and what that was all about. Keep them, so that in going

* *You're in Charge* [Chicago: Magnolia State Publishers, 1974.]

back over them you will see a record of your growth, and learn about yourself. You may get a sense of direction. It can be a map of the inner you.

Ira Progoff* has created a structured "Intensive Journal," in which one holds dialogues with different parts of one's environment and self. Art therapists Janie Rhyne† and Lucia Capacchione* both have suggested integrating drawing with writing to reach that nonverbal but very expressive part of ourselves.

Many feelings are hard to express in words. Poetry is more expressive than prose, especially when it does not rhyme, or even scan. Feelings are often easier to express through drawings, and with the use of color. Try using color; you may find that your answers have an added meaning for you. This is not an art book; do not be concerned with the aesthetics of your drawings, but, if the words do not come, pick a color and make a gesture or symbol expressing the feeling—the words will follow. Or just let the colors and lines speak for you.

Use this journal to keep a record of your thoughts and feelings, in words, pictures, and colors, as you go through school. It will be an invaluable record for you.

Such a journal can be used to understand yourself better. It can record what happened to you, how you felt about what happened, and, most important perhaps, what you learned from it about yourself. You can learn a lot about yourself by reflecting on your past, and how you came to be who you are. Here are some areas of your life you might wish to explore.

* *At a Journal Workshop.* (New York: Dialogue House Library, 1975).
† *The Gestalt Art Experience* (Monterey, Calif.: Brooks/Cole, 1974)
* *The Creative Journal* (Chicago. Swallow Press, 1979)

1. *Your family history.* Draw a picture of your family doing something. Where are you in the picture?

Draw a picture of each of your parents. Write a letter to each, telling them if they met your needs and expectations, and whether or not you are meeting theirs. Tell each of them how much love, security, and freedom there is in your relationship with them, and what you would like from them.

2. *Your development.* List the most important events, crises, transitions, changes, or developments in your life. Take time to do this because it should lead to a period of reflection on your life history. Draw pictures of those events that seem especially central to your life.

3. *Relationships.* Draw people. Draw your teachers as you sit in class. Draw your friends. Draw people you love. Draw people who anger you, or who make you feel bad. Let your drawing reflect how you feel about them.

4. *Enjoying life.* Draw five things you currently enjoy doing, that you do to play. Draw something you laughed about this week, or that made you feel good.

5. *Stress.* When you are under stress, pressure, or tension, where in your body do you experience it? How uncomfortable is the sensation? Draw situations that make you feel anxious, tense, depressed, fearful, or upset. Draw yourself under pressure. Draw your feelings. Draw a way of making yourself feel better.

Draw a picture depicting the symbolic relationship between your body, stress, any symptoms you may have, and your body's defenses. Which are the most powerful?

6. *Anger.* How do you feel when confronted by an angry person? What do you do? Draw an angry person. Who is it? What is that person angry about?

Where in your body do you experience your own anger? What do you do with it?

When you are having negative emotions, draw a series of pictures in your journal. Draw the emotion, using color and line to express the feeling. Draw a person having the emotion, a situation causing it, and what is getting in your way. Then draw symbolic solutions—the more violent, the better. You will not only feel better, it may clear the air and help you to work through to some realistic solutions.

7. *Personal identity.* Everyone has many identities which embody their attitudes about themselves and their relationship to others. Draw symbolic pictures of the different parts of yourself, that would answer the question, "Who am I?"

8. *Values.* Everyone derives some meaning and identity from the human community of which they are a part. A person might identify with many communities—professional, friendship networks, extended family, neighborhood, religion, ethnic group, political group, etc. Draw your communities, networks, and affiliations and something of their importance to you and your importance to them. How powerful do you feel in your community? How effective?

9. *The future.* What goals and achievements do you expect to accomplish? Draw them.

Imagine that you are being given a testimonial dinner on your next birthday. What are they saying about you? Write your own testimonial.

Imagine such a testimonial dinner on your one hundredth birthday. What are they saying about you? Write your own testimonial.

APPENDIX B
Jungian Types

SENSING TYPES

INTROVERTS

ISTJ

Serious, quiet, earn success by concentration and thoroughness. Practical, orderly, matter-of-fact, logical, realistic and dependable. See to it that everything is well organized. Take responsibility. Make up their own minds as to what should be accomplished and work toward it steadily, regardless of protests or distractions.

ISFJ

Quiet, friendly, responsible and conscientious. Work devotedly to meet their obligations and serve their friends and school. Thorough, painstaking, accurate. May need time to master technical subjects, as their interests are usually not technical. Patient with detail and routine. Loyal, considerate, concerned with how other people feel.

ISTP

Cool onlookers—quiet, reserved, observing and analyzing life with detached curiosity and unexpected flashes of original humor. Usually interested in impersonal principles, cause and effect, how and why mechanical things work. Exert themselves no more than they think necessary, because any waste of energy would be inefficient.

ISFP

Retiring, quietly friendly, sensitive, kind, modest about their abilities. Shun disagreements, do not force their opinions or values on others. Usually do not care to lead but are often loyal followers. Often relaxed about getting things done, because they enjoy the present moment and do not want to spoil it by undue haste or exertion.

E=extroverted; I=introverted; S=sensing; N=intuition; T=thinking; F=feeling; J=judgment; P=perception

With Each Type
Among Young People

INFJ

Succeed by perseverance, originality and desire to do whatever is needed or wanted. Put their best efforts into their work. Quietly forceful, conscientious, concerned for others. Respected for their firm principles. Likely to be honored and followed for their clear convictions as to how best to serve the common good.

INTJ

Usually have original minds and great drive for their own ideas and purposes. In fields that appeal to them, they have a fine power to organize a job and carry it through with or without help. Skeptical, critical, independent, determined, often stubborn. Must learn to yield less important points in order to win the most important.

INFP

Full of enthusiasms and loyalties, but seldom talk of these until they know you well. Care about learning, ideas, language, and independent projects of their own. Tend to undertake too much, then somehow get it done. Friendly, but often too absorbed in what they are doing to be sociable. Little concerned with possessions or physical surroundings.

INTP

Quiet, reserved, brilliant in exams, especially in theoretical or scientific subjects. Logical to the point of hair-splitting. Usually interested mainly in ideas, with little liking for parties or small talk. Tend to have sharply defined interests. Need to choose careers where some strong interest can be used and useful.

INTROVERTS

SENSING TYPES

EXTROVERTS

ESTP

Matter-of-fact, do not worry or hurry, enjoy whatever comes along. Tend to like mechanical things and sports, with friends on the side. May be a bit blunt or insensitive. Can do math or science when they see the need. Dislike long explanations. Are best with real things that can be worked, handled, taken apart or put together.

ESFP

Outgoing, easygoing, accepting, friendly, enjoy everything and make things more fun for others by their enjoyment. Like sports and making things. Know what's going on and join in eagerly. Find remembering facts easier than mastering theories. Are best in situations that need sound common sense and practical ability with people as well as with things.

ESTJ

Practical, realistic, matter-of-fact, with a natural head for business or mechanics. Not interested in subjects they see no use for, but can apply themselves when necessary. Like to organize and run activities. May make good administrators, especially if they remember to consider others' feelings and points of view.

ESFJ

Warm-hearted, talkative, popular, conscientious, born cooperators, active committee members. Need harmony and may be good at creating it. Always doing something nice for someone. Work best with encouragement and praise. Little interest in abstract thinking or technical subjects. Main interest is in things that directly and visibly affect people's lives.

With Each Type
Among Young People

INTUITIVE TYPES*

ENFP	ENTP
Warmly enthusiastic, high-spirited, ingenious, imaginative. Able to do almost anything that interests them. Quick with a solution for any difficulty and ready to help anyone with a problem. Often rely on their ability to improvise instead of preparing in advance. Can usually find compelling reasons for whatever they want.	Quick, ingenious, good at many things. Stimulating company, alert and outspoken. May argue for fun on either side of a question. Resourceful in solving new and challenging problems, but may neglect routine assignments. Apt to turn to one new interest after another. Skillful in finding logical reasons for what they want.
ENFJ	**ENTJ**
Responsive and responsible. Generally feel real concern for what others think or want, and try to handle things with due regard for other people's feelings. Can present a proposal or lead a group discussion with ease and tact. Sociable, popular, active in school affairs, but put time enough on their studies to do good work.	Hearty, frank, able in studies, leaders in activities. Usually good in anything that requires reasoning and intelligent talk, such as public speaking. Are usually well-informed and enjoy adding to their fund of knowledge. May sometimes be more positive and confident than their experience in an area warrants.

EXTROVERTS

* Reproduced by special permission of the publisher, Consulting Psychologist Press, Inc,. Palo Alto, CA 94306 from *Manual: A Guide to the Development of the Myers Briggs Type Indicator* by Isabel Briggs Myers and Mary H. McCaulley © 1985.

Index

abortion, 41–42
acceptance, social, 29–30
Acquired Immune Deficiency
    Syndrome (AIDS), 47
addictions, 168–69, 171–72
    and anger, 196
advice, 17–18
    see also criticism
affirming, 56–57, 94

aggressiveness:
    and assertiveness, 86
    and criticism, 112–13
AIDS Related Diseases (ARD),
    47
alcohol, 19, 156, 168–69
    and depression, 217
    and sexual dysfunction, 44,
    46

anger, 191–214
  and anxiety, 198
  communicating, 204–5
  coping with others', 206–13
  coping with your own,
    199–206
  dexifying to an angry person,
    209–10
  erroneous concepts about,
    196–98
  expressing, 199–200
  and frustration, 194
  physical reactions to, 193–94
  recording in a journal, 262–63
  running away from, 207
  and sexual dysfunction,
    44–46
  submitting to, 208–9
  what do we do with, 194–96
anorexia nervosa, 170
antidepressants, 217
anxiety, 173–90
  and anger, 198
  and assertiveness, 86–87
  body's reactions to, 189–90
  causes of, 174–76, 177–78
  and confidence, 121–24
  coping with, 184–89
  effects of, 184–85
  and exams, 180–89
  and fear, 173–74
  "free-floating," 176
  as inefficient, 177
  and the inner critic, 108–109
  and motivation, 146–48
  performance, 17, 82, 124,
    178–79
  and separation, 22–23, 32–35

  and sexual dysfunction,
    44–46
  using food to reduce, 170–71
  see also feelings
apologizing, 209–10
appearance, "looking good," 16,
    26–27
assertiveness, 85–88
  attempts to divert, 96–99
  broken record, 94
  and depression, 223–25
  and hearing "no," 99
  and insults, 98
  learning, 88–89
  and questions, 96–97
  in the real world, 99–100
  and self-esteem, 17, 85
  Subjective Units of
    Discomfort, 89–91
  and threats, 97–98
attack, as a response to feelings,
    167
authenticity, 25–26

Bandler, Richard, 34, 85
Benson, Herbert, 188
birth control, 42–44
blaming, 194–95
Bogen, Joseph, 234–35, 237
"boo," 168
Bowlby, John, 33
brain, two functions of, 233,
    237–38, 243–44
  left, 233, 235–37, 240
  right, 225, 233, 234–37, 240,
    250–52
  right-brain people in a
    left-brain world, 249–250

breathing, and anxiety, 185
Briggs, Katherine, 67, 68, 70
broken record, 94–96, 113
bulemia, 170–71
bull sessions, 53
burn-out, 18, 151–52

candor, 25–26
Capacchione, Lucia, 261
career-oriented students, 133–34
careers, and connections, 29–30
centering meditation, 188–89
chlamydia, 47
cigarettes, 168
colds, and homesickness, 22
competence:
    and exam anxiety, 181–82
    projecting an air of, 26
    and superiority, 151–52
compulsiveness, 127–28
    and addiction, 168–69
    and bad feelings, 167
conditioning, 129–30, 147
condoms, 44, 47
confidence, 118–25
    projecting an air of, 26
    and structure, 126–28
connections, making, 29–30
content-process shift, 114–15
contraception, 42–44
conversations, 50–52
    and affirming, 56
    and being right, 59–60
    changing the level of, 58–59
    and free information, 55
    and kinds of listening, 54–59
    questions in, 59
    and reflection, 60

and self-disclosure, 57
sharing thoughts and feelings
    through, 53
as trivia contests, 51, 53
coping skills, 14
creative, 226–27
and fantasy vs. reality, 229
and homesickness, 23
and stress, 19–20
counseling centers, college,
    19–20
    and long-term depression, 217
courses, safe, 128–29
Creative Journal, The
    (Capacchione), 259n
creativity, 226–52
    and brain functions, 233–39,
        250–52
    characteristics of creative
        people, 229–32
    and children, 239–40, 250–51
    and imagery, 244–48
    removing blocks to, 240–43
    and unconventional thinking,
        229–32
criticism, 102–17
    accepting, 17–18
    constructive vs. destructive,
        112–17
    and creativity, 240–41
    desensitization, 116
    "dexifying," 110, 113
    guilt, 107–8
    and hostility, 113–15
    inner, 108–9
    messages contained in, 103–4
    and parents, 105–7
    reducing fear of, 109–11

decisions, 16
    and feelings, 163
    and self-esteem, 81–83
defensiveness:
    and criticism, 103, 111–12, 113
    "dexifying," 110, 113, 209–10
    see also assertiveness
denial, of feelings, 166–67
dependency, in relationships,
    32, 35, 77–78
depression, 215–25
    and anger, 196
    long-term, 217
    preventing, 219–25
    and separation, 22–23
    short-term, 216–17
    suicidal, 218–19
desensitization, 116
dexifying, 110
    to an angry person, 209–10
    and hostile, critical remarks,
    113
differences, comparing, 66–67
disabilities, learning, 150
diseases, sexually transmitted,
    44, 47
displacement, 195
dreams, 75
drugs, 19, 157, 169
    and depression, 217
    rehabilitation, 171–72
dumping, 195
dyslexia, 150

enjoyment:
    and anxiety, 146–47
    of classes and subjects,
    152–53

and studying, 134–36,
    141–42, 146–47
Erickson, Milton, 74
exam anxiety, coping with,
    180–89
    see also anxiety
exercises:
    anchoring good feelings,
    84–85
    assertiveness, 92–96
    clay and process, 153–54
    comparing differences, 66–67
    coping with hostile, critical
    people, 113–15
    creative imagery, 244–47
    crossing a chasm, 228–29
    exploring your unconscious,
    75–77
    identity, 64–65
    reducing fear of criticism,
    109–11
    reflecting, 60–61
    separation and grief, 33–35
    two animals, 248–49
    your inner child, 36–37
expectations:
    parents', 123–24
    reviewing and revising your,
    222–23
experience, learning from,
    111–12
external rewards, 138–40
extroversion and extroverts,
    68–69, 268–69

failures:
    and anxiety, 181–82
    formula for, 258

fantasy, 229
  see also brain, two functions
    of
fear, and anxiety, 173–75, 176
feelings, 18–19, 155–72
  accepting, 223–24
  and anxiety, 186, 187
  coping with, 158–60, 161–64
  and creativity, 243
  and feelers, 70, 71
  hiding, 26–27
  and logic, 156
  about loneliness, 24
  meanings of, 159–60
  self-destructive ways of
    dealing with, 166–72
  about separation, 23
  sharing, 53
  and shyness, 165–66
  types of, 160–61
  using, 161–63
  about yourself, 16–17, 84–85
  see also self-esteem
fogging, 115
food, and anxiety, 170–71
free information, 55
frustration, and anger, 194

gay culture, 48
Gazzaniga, Michael, 236
Gestalt Art Experience, The
  (Rhyne), 261
goals:
  and burn-out, 151
  and career-oriented students,
    133–34
  and pathways, 254–57
  and self-esteem, 81–82

gonorrhea, 47
*Go See the Movies in Your
  Head* (Shorr), 75
grades, 16–17
  as external rewards, 138–40
  and loss of confidence,
    123–24
  and self-esteem, 181, 220
grief, 33–34
Grinder, John, 34, 85
groups, joining, 28–29
guilt, 107–8

headaches:
  and anger, 199
  and anxiety, 184
  and homesickness, 22
herpes, 47
Hesse, Herman, 255
heterosexuality, 48
homesickness, 16, 22–23, 220
homosexuality, 48–49
honesty, 25–26
hostility, and criticism, 112–16
hypnotism, 74

image, projecting an, 26–27
imagery, 244–48
information, free, 55
inhibitions, sexual, 39
inner child, 35–37
  and intellectual stimulation,
    134–35
  and procrastination, 144
inner critic, 108–109
insecurity, 124–25
  and the "right" way, 129–31
  see also criticism; self-esteem

insults, and assertiveness, 98
intellectually stimulated
    students, 134–36
internal rewards, 139–40
introversion and introverts,
    68–69, 266–67
intuitives, 69–70, 267, 269
"invulnerables," 82–83

joking, about feelings, 166–67
journal, keeping a, 225, 259–63
Jung, Carl, 67, 68, 69
Jungian Types, 67–73, 265–69

Kansky, Jacqueline, 38
King Solomon's Ring (Lorenz),
    130

learning:
    disabilities, 150
    early, and self-esteem, 81–82
    from experience, 111–12
    operant conditioning theory
        of, 129–30
learning disabilities, 150
listening, 50–61
    and being right, 59–60
    for free information, 55
    kinds of conversations, 53
    questions, 59
    ways of, 54–59
    see also conversations
lists, 149
loneliness, 24
    and conversations, 51
    and shyness, 27
Long-Term Best Interests
    (LTBI), 140

looking good, 16, 26–27
Lorenz, Konrad, 130
love, falling in, 16
    first love affair, 31–32,
        221–22

Marx, Groucho, 30–31
May, Rollo, 252
meditation, 75, 186–88
men:
    and contraception, 43–44
    and sexual dysfunction, 45
    and sexual orientation, 48
Miller, Alice, 195
mirroring, 54–55, 60
motivation, 132–54
    and anxiety, 146–48
    and burning out, 18, 151–52
    doing what comes easy,
        152–53
    external rewards, 138–40
    fear as, 182
    and kinds of students, 133–
        38
    and learning to enjoy work,
        141–42
    and process, 153–54
    and procrastination, 143–45
    and resistance, 142–45
muscles:
    relaxing, 185, 200
    spasms, and anger, 199
Myers, Isabel, 67, 68, 244
Myers-Briggs test, 67

networks, 24–25
nurturing, 32–33
    yourself, 35–37

operant conditioning, 129–130, 147

orgasm, 46

Ornstein, Robert, 188

parents:
  and criticism, 105–8
  expectations, 123–24
  and guilt, 107–8
  problems of, 220–21
  rules of, 15–16
  separation from, 22–23

passive-aggressiveness, 143, 195–96

pathways, 254–58

people:
  and groups, 28
  how to meet, 25
  see also relationships

perfectionism, 144–45

performance anxiety, 17, 82, 124, 178–79

personalities, Jungian Types of, 67–73

phony, reputation for being a, 25

Plato Society (UCLA), 136

pregnancy, unwanted, 41–42
  avoiding, 42–44

prejudices, discovering, 28

problems, 14–15

process, 14–15, 114–15, 153–54

procrastination, 143–44

Progoff, Ira, 261

Psychology of Consciousness, The (Ornstein), 188

questions, open-ended, 59

Rainwater, Jan, 259–60

reality, 229
  see also brain, two functions of

relationships:
  the Groucho Marx club, 30–31
  and homesickness, 23
  and honesty, 25–26
  insecurity in, 125
  and listening, 50–52
  and loneliness, 24
  networks, 24–25
  recording in a journal, 262
  and separation anxiety, 32–35
  see also sex

Relaxation Response, The (Benson), 188

relevance, and motivation, 136–38

rejection, practicing, 165–66

repression, 196

resistance, 142–45

rewards:
  creativity as its own, 241
  external, 138–40
  internal, 139–40

Rhyne, Janie, 261

Rotter, Julian, 80

running, and anxiety, 187

safety, 128–31

self-awareness, 62–78
  and assertiveness, 85–95
  and differences from others, 65–69
  and identity, 64–65

self-awareness (*continued*)
  Jungian personality types, 67–73
  unconscious, 73–77
  valuing your individuality, 77–78
self-disclosure, 25–26, 57–58
self-esteem, 79–100
  and anxiety, 174–76
  and competence, 151–52
  and creativity, 240
  and criticism, 17–18, 117
  and depression, 220, 223
  and goals, 80–81, 124
  and grades, 182, 220
  improving, 83–85
  sources of, 81–83
  see also assertiveness
sensates, 69, 70
separation anxiety, 22–23, 32–35
  and first love affair, 32
  and grief, 33–34
sex and sexuality, 38–40
  becoming a non-virgin, 40–41
  casual, 49
  contraception, 42–44
  dysfunctions, 44–46
  mixed signals from society about, 16, 39
  and pregnancy, 41–42
  safe, 47
  and sexually transmitted diseases, 47
  sexual orientation, 48–49
Shorr, Joseph E., 75, 77
shyness, 27, 164–66
Siddhartha (Hesse), 255

Skinner, B. F., 147
Smith, Jack, 70
social competence and success, 29–30
Soul of a New Machine, The (Kidder), 242
specialization, too much, 129
Sperry, Roger, 233–34, 235, 236, 237, 243
stomachaches, and homesickness, 22
stress:
  coping with, 19–20
  and dependency, 78
  recording in a journal, 260–61
structure, 126–28
  study habits, 148–50
Structure of Magic, The (Bandler and Grinder), 34
studying:
  to avoid anxiety, 146–48
  and exam anxiety, 180–81
  habits, 148–50
  and motivation, 18, 140–41
Subjective Units of Discomfort (SUDS), 89–92
success, formula for, 258
suicide, 19, 218
  see also depression
superiority, 151–52
support groups and systems, 28, 221
suppression, of feelings, 166–67
syphilis, 47

thinking and thinkers, 70–72
  unconventional, 229–32

Thou Shalt Not Be Aware
(Miller), 194n
threats, and assertiveness, 97–98
time:
   budgeting, 148–49
   consciousness, 243
   and exam anxiety, 180–81
trivia contests, conversations as, 51, 53

unconscious, 73–77

vaginismus, 46
venereal warts, 47
virginity, 40–41

women:
   and contraception, 43
   and pregnancy, 42
   and sexual dysfunction, 46
   and sexual orientation, 48–49
word processors, 145
work, enjoying, 135–36, 141–42
Wozniak, Steve, 227

YOUR PERSONAL JOURNAL